Introducing Malaguzzi

Sandra Smidt offers a good introduction, both accessible and comprehensive, to the early childhood education of Reggio Emilia and the pedagogical ideas and practice of Loris Malaguzzi, one of the great educators of the last century. Like the Reggio project itself, [this] book is a provocation to the thinking and practice that dominates the field ... showing there are alternatives.

Professor Emeritus Peter Moss, Institute of Education,
University of London

In this accessible and engaging text, Sandra Smidt examines how Malaguzzi's philosophy developed out of his personal experiences of growing up in post-fascist Italy. His ideas are explored and illustrated throughout by examples relating to everyday early years practice. The key themes explored include:

- relationships – the importance of relationships, culture and contexts to learning within any setting and beyond;
- transparency – the importance of listening and documentation to understanding and sharing learning;
- questioning – inviting children to not only answer questions but raise them, allowing them to be equal partners in all learning situations;
- creativity – enabling children to use all the expressive languages they can find to express and share their ideas;
- equity and fairness – involving the community in all decision making and discussions, to ensure that early childhood education is accessible and relevant to *all* children.

This book will be of benefit to all those working with young children and essential reading for students on early childhood education programmes.

Sandra Smidt is a writer and consultant in early years education. Her most recent titles include *Introducing Bruner* (2011) and *Introducing Vygotsky* (2008), both published by Routledge.

Other titles available

Introducing Malaguzzi

Exploring the life and work of
Reggio Emilia's founding father

Sandra Smidt

Routledge
Taylor & Francis Group

LONDON AND NEW YORK

First published 2013
by Routledge
2 Park Square, Milton Park, Abingdon, Oxon OX14 4RN

Simultaneously published in the USA and Canada
by Routledge
711 Third Avenue, New York, NY 10017

Routledge is an imprint of the Taylor & Francis Group, an informa business

British Library Cataloguing in Publication Data
A catalogue record for this book is available from the British Library

Library of Congress Cataloging in Publication Data
Smidt, Sandra, 1943–
Introducing Malaguzzi : exploring the life and work of Reggio Emilia's
founding father / Sandra Smidt.
 p. cm.
 1. Malaguzzi, Loris, 1920-1994. 2. Educators--Italy--Biography.
 3. Reggio Emilia approach (Early childhood education) I. Title.
 LB880.M3152S65 2012   370.92--dc23[B]
 2012019574

ISBN: 978-0-415-52498-8 (hbk)
ISBN: 978-0-415-52501-5 (pbk)
ISBN: 978-0-203-11185-7 (ebk)

Typeset in Galliard and Gill Sans
by Bookcraft Ltd, Stroud, Gloucestershire

MIX
Paper from
responsible sources
FSC® C004839

Printed and bound in Great Britain by
TJ International Ltd, Padstow, Cornwall

This book is dedicated to my children and my children's children, with all my love. Written during a time of depression and recession, I hope it is imbued with the vision some people had when setting up the wonderful provision for young children in Reggio Emilia during another dark phase of European history.

Contents

Introduction
Context and culture

> Word had it that at Villa Cella, the people had gotten together to put up a school for the young children: they had pulled out the bricks from the bombed-out houses and had used them to build the walls of the school. Only a few days had passed since the Liberation and everything was still violently topsy-turvy ... I got on my bicycle and rode out to Villa Cella. I got confirmation from a farmer just outside the village; he pointed out the place, a long way ahead. There were piles of sand and of bricks, a wheelbarrow full of hammers, shovels and hoes ... I was excited by the way it overturned logic and prejudices, the old rules governing pedagogy, culture, how it forced everything back to the beginning. It opened up completely new horizons of thought ...
>
> (Malaguzzi in Edwards *et al.* 2011: 27–8)

In 2009 Routledge published the first in what has become a series of books looking at the work of some great thinkers and innovators in the field of child development. The first book, *Introducing Vygotsky*, examined the thinking of the great Russian theorist who died young but, in his short life, contributed an enormous amount to what we understand about how children learn, particularly about the importance of context, culture, language, history and the role of others in learning and development. Vygotsky's thinking had an enormous influence on me and my work, and the book was written for that very reason. One of the aims behind the writing of it was to make Vygotsky's concepts accessible to a non-academic audience. His ideas are difficult, and made more so through the sometimes florid and complex translations from the original Russian. My audience is primarily teachers, teaching assistants, students and those working in various roles in early years education and care. The book was well received and has since, surprisingly, been translated into Danish.

Not long afterwards, I wrote a companion book, *Introducing Bruner*. This seemed a natural progression, not only in that Bruner had been much influenced by Vygotsky and the importance of the sociocultural in learning, but also because his interest in language led him to explore in great detail the importance of narrative as a key tool in both making and sharing meaning. As you almost certainly know, the roles of language and narrative in early learning are extremely significant.

The subject of this third book in the series is the Italian thinker and teacher, Loris Malaguzzi, the founder of the the Reggio Emilia preschools programmes that have become so well known. Although not, perhaps, as much of a founding father as Vygotsky or Bruner, he was able to combine the idealism that grew out of his own life experiences with a steady pragmatism, and a growing knowledge and understanding of the importance of offering high-quality interpersonal early childhood experiences and development to the life of a whole community. The purpose of this book is therefore to explore how Malaguzzi, drawing on the ideas of Vygotsky and Bruner, amongst others, added his own particular post-war Italian experience to refine and broaden our understanding of how children learn, and to suggest what adults can do to foster and enhance this learning and development.

It is likely that some of you reading this book will already know something about Reggio Emilia and the work that started there, as the easy sharing of information via the internet has made it possible for the fame of this preschool system to spread. Books about and from Reggio Emilia are being published all the time; some highly relevant, others less so. It could even be argued that the very fame of the system is what has led to it being copied without being fully understood.

As one of those fortunate enough to have visited Reggio Emilia and its preschools, and to have met and talked with Malaguzzi himself, many years ago, I came to recognise that there is need for a new book to hone in on the underpinning ideas, philosophy and research behind the 'fame' of Reggio Emilia. For me, the essential question to consider is what it was that made it possible for Malaguzzi not only to arrive at his ideas, but also to work so closely with local people to make sure they become reality. The Reggio preschools are particularly famous for the wonderful artwork produced by the children. Because the children's drawings and paintings are easy to reproduce in books, postcards, posters or online, they are widely available to be admired. It became clear to me that many people involved with young children, and seeing this and perhaps visiting the preschools themselves in real life or on screens, began to think it might be relatively simple to adopt or copy what they have seen in their own settings.

For me, the very essence of the Reggio Emilia preschools is rooted in their history, culture and contexts. Reggio Emilia offers no recipes, blueprints or models. It has no curriculum we can follow, nor is there any teacher training programme to replicate. What I plan to do in this book is to analyse what has been done and why, in order that we can learn to use our own history, culture and contexts to create and improve our early years settings.

So the question for me and for you is whether something developed in response to the history of one place can be successfully transferred to another. Vygotsky, Bruner and Malaguzzi were each the product of their life and times, and in order to understand them and their ideas we have to adopt a sociocultural/historical approach. Context and culture are essential to our understanding. So this is where our journey begins.

You will notice that this is a book without any illustrations. It was, of course, enormously tempting to ask for permission to use some of the wonderful art produced by the children in Reggio Emilia, but since this is a book about the processes rather than the products, I decided to refrain.

My thanks go to Annamaria Mucchi who unfailingly and generously provided answers to my questions.

Notes

- I use 'she' rather than 'he' when referring to individual children.
- Following the work of Dahlberg and Moss, I use the terms used by them in accordance with accepted practice in Reggio Emilia. There are two main types of early childhood service: the *nido* (nest), which is a centre for children of about 3 months up to 3 years, and the *scuola dell'infanzia*, which is a centre or nursery school for children from 3 years up to the compulsory school age of 6 years. In Reggio, both types of setting are called municipal schools. When I talk of overall provision for children below school age I sometimes use the term preschool.
- I decided to use the word 'teacher' rather than practitioner to refer to all adults in settings working with children, since this is what is done in Reggio Emilia. This is in recognition of the fact that all those who encounter the children affect their learning and development, and teach them in some way.
- I use the word 'municipality' to mean the equivalent of our local authority.
- Two additional terms are used to refer to educators. There are *pedagogisti*, who have a higher degree in pedagogy or psychology and work with a small number of municipal schools to help develop their thinking about pedagogy and issues arising from that. We might call such people 'advisory teachers'. There are also *atelieristi*, who have a background in the visual arts, work in the studio or atelier in the settings and play a vital role in the learning and development of the children. We have no equivalent in English.
- I choose to use English rather than American spelling for words translated from Italian, so you will find theatre rather than theater and so on.
- There is no curriculum (or *programmazione*) in place in the provision in Reggio. What happens is more responsive, more open-ended and more culturally based. The Italian word *progettazione* is used. This word has many meanings, including to design, plan or devise or project. The word is sometimes translated as project work (as in the work of Lillian Katz), but it has a much broader and more global meaning.

Chapter 1

The life and times of Loris Malaguzzi

World War II, or any war, in its tragic absurdity might have been the kind of experience that pushes a person towards the job of educating, as a way to start anew and live and work for the future. This desire strikes a person, as the war finally ends and the symbols of life reappear with violence equal to that of the time of destruction. ... Right after the war I felt a pact, an alliance with children, adults, veterans from prison camps, partisans of the Resistance, and the sufferers of a devastated world.

(Malaguzzi in Edwards *et al.* 2011: 35)

We know that Loris Malaguzzi was born in Correggio, a small town and commune near Reggio Emilia in the province of Emilia Romagna, in the valley of the River Po. We know that he was born in 1920 and lived until 1994. We know that he married a woman named Nilde Bonaccini, who died in 1993. He died six weeks later at the age of only 74. We know that they had one son. Apart from that, we know almost nothing about his family, where they lived, what work they did, what their loves, passions, interests and fears were, or what they believed in and valued.

We do know that he grew up during the time of Benito Mussolini's Fascist rule and that this was extremely significant to his thinking and development. He said that fascism had 'gobbled up my youth'(Brunson 2001). With the encouragement of his father, he chose to become a teacher and enrolled in a teacher-training institute in 1939, from where he qualified as a primary teacher. After the war he enrolled in a course in Rome, studying psychology, at the National Centre for Research. This was, in fact, the first post-war course in psychology in Italy. After that he worked as a teacher in a state primary school for seven years. He was often described as being a polymath because of his wide range of interests, talents and abilities. These included being a sportsman, a theatre director, a maker of films and a journalist.

After his time in Rome he returned to Reggio Emilia, where he worked for the municipality (which you will remember is the equivalent of our local authorities) in a centre for children experiencing learning difficulties at school

– a coincidental link with Vygotsky, who had also spent some of his too-short life working with children with special needs. In 1958 he became director of preschools in Reggio Emilia, where he spent the rest of his working life. He retired officially in 1985 but continued to dedicate all his energy to the system he had helped to create until his early death.

It seems strange that we know so little about his personal life, compared to what we know about the lives of Bruner and Vygotsky. What we do know something about is the culture and the context of his life, which we can usefully examine in order to understand and explain the effect they had on his thinking. In doing so we are adopting a socio-historical/cultural approach as we explore the history of Reggio Emilia and its inevitable impact on Loris Malaguzzi. You will appreciate that this is a vast area so, of necessity, this will be something of a potted history, but it will enable us to analyse just what it was that happened to Malaguzzi to have so profoundly affected his thinking, his philosophy, his questions and his answers.

You may feel tempted at this point to skip the rest of this chapter, thinking you want to know more about his ideas and less about history or politics. But I urge you to read what follows with attention because, without an understanding of this, you will not be able to really appreciate what makes Reggio Emilia so important and, for many people, so very elusive. To understand the preschool provision in Reggio Emilia you do have to understand the context.

A brief overview of the political history of Italy

The history of the small city of Reggio Emilia is that of many small cities in Europe, marked primarily by the physical devastation of intensive bombing, invasion, division, hatred, patriotism, guerrilla activity, subjugation and ultimate victory. The suffering of the people was so intense that there existed a state of almost civil war between the factions of those who had supported Mussolini and the fascists and those who had opposed him. It is difficult for people whose country has never been invaded to understand the depth of feeling that developed.

The defining event of the French Revolution in 1789 brought about massive changes in Europe. The development of industry, together with the move of people from the countryside to urban centres and the creation of a laissez-faire market economy, began to change many of the existing structures and groupings throughout much of Europe.

Fifty years later, in 1848, Karl Marx and Frederick Engels wrote *The Communist Manifesto*, proclaiming that the working class would rise, engage in class struggle, undo the gains of the bourgeoisie and control the means of production. The effect of this would be to end the marginalisation and alienation of groups of people, and bring about a fairer and more equitable society.

The political climate of Italy grew out of the parallel development of two opposing and powerful ideologies, socialism/communism (based on the ideas of Marx and Engels) and fascism. In 1892 the Italian Socialist Party (*Partita Socialista d'Italia PSI*) was founded in Genoa. Italy had been on the winning side of the 1914–18 world war, although that victory was painfully earned. It was tinged with resentment when Italy appeared to make fewer gains than the other winning countries; one of the things that most angered the people was the awarding of the town of Fiume to then-called Yugoslavia and, after an abortive attempt to take back Fiume, Italians talked angrily of their 'mutilated victory'. In the succeeding years there were some political changes moving from a system dominated by small cliques to a fully fledged parliamentary democracy. In the 1919 elections the dominant parties were the Socialists and the Catholic People's Party. The Socialists were optimistic but the party subsequently (and disastrously as it turned out) split into two factions – the Trades Union faction led by Filippo Tulati and the International Socialist faction led by the young Benito Mussolini.

The PSI was initially opposed to Italy becoming involved in the war, which led to Mussolini leaving the party and later, disenchanted by the state of post-war Italy, to form his own, the Fascist Party.

It is important to understand what it was that the opposing political groups stood for:

- Fascism was and still is an extreme right-wing party, glorifying one race or nation above all others. It is, by definition and history, opposed to communism or liberalism and hence hostile towards all those struggling to free themselves from oppression. These include women, workers, immigrants, the poor, the voiceless, the vote-less and children. It is important to learn and to remember that the Catholic Church in Italy supported Mussolini, his party and his policies, and this, as we will see, became very significant to how Malaguzzi's thinking developed.
- The communists/socialists in Italy have had a checkered and difficult history, with the formation of factions within and then smaller groupings within those very factions, opposition from without and lack of effective leadership. Traditionally their interest has been in liberating those who are voiceless and oppressed by considering the provision of education, work and opportunities for all. For all their difficulties they have had some serious and important leaders.

One of the most interesting of these was Antonio Gramsci. He became a leading thinker on many things, including education and schooling. He was a Marxist and a journalist, who was incarcerated by the fascists and spent the last 11 years of his life in one of Mussolini's prisons. During this time he smuggled out his now-famous notebooks/diaries, which have since been published and become extremely powerful and influential documents.

Although the diaries were published promptly in Italy, they only appeared in English translation in the 1970s. He had been born in a small town on the island of Sardinia in 1891 and was one of seven children. His was one of the few literate families on the island; he excelled at school and won a scholarship to the University of Torino, a city in the north of Italy, sometimes called 'the red capital of Italy'. By the end of the First World War Torino's population was made up of 30 per cent industrial workers, excluding the 10 per cent who were in the army. The workers of Torino had a very combative history and it was in this world, this atmosphere and culture, that Gramsci started his university life. He was already a socialist and, over time, began to consider the importance of the struggle against bourgeois (or what we might call middle class) values. For him, this struggle for equality was an ideological and cultural one. One of his key ideas is that of *hegemony*, which is how the whole of any society is permeated by a system of values, beliefs, attitudes and morals that has the effect of supporting and maintaining the status quo in power relations. So, for example, in Italy during the fascist years, the values of the Catholic Church, upholding the values of the fascists, ensured that little or nothing changed. In essence, hegemony is inseparable from power. When you start to consider Malaguzzi's values and principles you will begin to have more of an understanding of what is meant by hegemony.

The communists and socialists, with their commitment to social change designed to rectify the existing unfairness, wanted better provision for the children of the poor, for women and girls, for children largely unseen. In doing this they began to think about and later to debate a number of issues. These included the following:

- The question of whether educators should have particular specialist training and what this should consist of and how it should be delivered.
- What children should learn and where and how.
- How to build an education around not just knowing what others have said, thought and done, but essentially about questioning what has been said, thought and done. This became a key theme in Malaguzzi's thinking, as you will see.

The politics of Reggio Emilia

Reggio Emilia itself is a small and beautiful town. It has fine architecture, paved streets, historic buildings, squares and open spaces, a tiny theatre and what is called the best preschool provision for young children in the world. It was where the Italian flag, the tricolour, was first unveiled. It is set in the rich agricultural and industrial region of Emilia Romagna – an area sometimes called Italy's 'red belt' or *zona rosa*, because it was here that the majority of the people, poor and exploited, joined the socialist and communist parties that later led the resistance to the German Occupation during the Second World War.

The region suffered terribly during this war. There was fierce fighting, vicious reprisals and great suffering and injustice, which touched and coloured the lives of all. An analysis of the period suggests that the growth and strength of the resistance during the war continued beyond it to create social, political, institutional and cultural breaks with the past. The region had for generations been dominated by a civil and class war between the landlords and wealthy (who had often been supporters of fascism) and the labourers, farmhands and the poor.

After the war, trades unions developed and gained more power, and the vital role the communists had played in ensuring liberation allowed them to begin winning electoral victories in the first local elections, then to build links with other social actors and, in some cases, with the Anglo-Americans, who had come into the region with the express purpose of supervising the building of what they called 'democracy' in Italy. It is clear that the devastation of war had caused the infrastructure to be badly damaged, unemployment was high, food was rationed and there was a growing black market. Agriculture, the most important sector of the economy, was marked by backwardness and the effects of low consumption. The people had little to live on.

The period between the end of the war and 1955 is sometimes described as a 'phase of learning'. What is meant by this is that it was seen as the time when the communists learned by doing. Their aim was to achieve social change and, in seeking this, they were both pragmatic and ideological. In short, they did things that they could do practically, politically and economically, but also things that they believed to be right or just. They set about trying to improve the living conditions of the working class, modifying the economic structures and the social dynamics, as well as, surprisingly, intensifying their support of capitalist development.

For Malaguzzi, there were lessons to be learned from what was happening in his community to its inhabitants. He was party to the things the communists were trying and able to do, and ideologically his heart was with their goals and ambitions. He learned that he, too, could learn from the things he began to do. This meant that he felt able to start trying to change things before he had been specifically trained to do so. He also learned that, in order to achieve his goals, he, like the communists, needed to be both pragmatic and ideological. These are difficult and sometimes contradictory ideas but, as we trace what Malaguzzi did, you will be able to assess just how pragmatic and idealistic he would remain.

So we know that Malaguzzi's childhood and early adulthood were spent under the shadow of fascism, and that he was alive to see the effects of both fascism and war on the people around him. He directly experienced the hunger, the poverty, the damage to the infrastructure of his communities, the rations, the attacks on learning and thinking and reading and questioning. His experiences allowed him to become critical of the dominance of the church in early education and gave him an awareness of the vital and varied roles played by trades unionists, peasants, workers, factory owners, officials, women, mothers, educators, politicians and others.

The history of early childhood education in Reggio Emilia up to 1945

Having looked briefly at the history of Italy, particularly at the growth of both communism and fascism, and its impact on the life and thoughts of Malaguzzi, we now narrow the focus to look at the early development of provision for young children in the region up to the end of the Second World War, around when Malaguzzi emerged as a trained teacher.

Interest in national provision for the care and education of young children has a long history. During the decade of Italy's unification in the nineteenth century, the president of the national association of *Asili Rurali per L'infanzia* (rural care for young children) went to ask the king to support the development of some preschool provision. In addition, the Catholic Church sponsored out-of-home care for disadvantaged preschool children in the form of charitable social service and religious training for much of the nineteenth and twentieth centuries. For most Italians, however, and for much of the twentieth century, a collaborative model of home-based child care had been the norm and the ideal. Responsibility for the care of the young child, particularly of infants and toddlers, was considered a family responsibility, involving both nuclear and extended family members, generally women.

At the beginning of the twentieth century there were some significant developments in thinking about early childhood education in Italy in general. In the more industrialised regions, some communities and private entrepreneurs began to experiment with organised child care for children before they reached school age.

In 1907, Maria Montessori set up the first *Casa dei Bambini* (Children's House) in the slums of San Lorenzo in Rome. There she experimented with the methods and equipment she had developed with and for children with disabilities. Observation, individualism and auto-education were the watchwords of her approach. In 1912, an English edition of her book, *The Montessori Method*, was published, making her internationally famous. She created a second *Casa dei Bambini* in Milan and, not long afterwards, mothers in that city began to demand provision for preschool children to enable them to go to work. In 1924 she made the mistake, in my view, of accepting government support for her methods. Ten years later she refused to concede further to Mussolini's demands and he insisted that all Montessori schools throughout the country be closed. The same fate befell the schools she set up in Germany when Hitler came to power. It is interesting that a process of looking at and listening to the children, seeing them as individuals and focusing on how they could take control of their own learning was so threatening. Think about this as you carry on reading.

Also influential in their way were the two sisters, Rosa and Caroline Agazzi, who developed some new ideas about how to teach children and train teachers. They were interested in how young children used what they called their 'natural abilities' to express themselves when they were in situations closely resembling the home. You might wonder if there is any such thing as 'the home' and whether some homes were, and sometimes still are, regarded as superior to others. You might also wonder if their ideas on education had anything to do with learning.

Looking more closely and regionally at Reggio Emilia, we know that the area had suffered tremendous losses during the First World War and its economy lay in ruins afterwards. Thousands were without work, and it was during this phase that Benito Mussolini (originally a member of the communist party) became disillusioned with the communists and set up his rival fascist party. In 1922 the king asked him to form a government, which he did and where he remained until he was deposed in 1943. Perhaps you will not be surprised to learn that Mussolini was impressed with the views of the Agazzi sisters and, under him, a system of state-run ONMI services (National Organisation for Mothers and Infants) was established from 1925 for the care and support of children in large, poor families. It was during this dreadful time in power that he instituted what were called the *Gentile Reforms* to the education systems. These required that education for children under the age of 6 was not compulsory and, during the fascist era, became the responsibility of the Catholic Church. In fact, this system of education, approved of by the Church, became official state policy. In 1925 an iniquitous law called *Protection and Assistance in Infancy* was passed, which insisted on state support for large families, in line with Mussolini's aim of increasing the population.

So this was the system in place when Malaguzzi began to think about making his life's work teaching and learning.

A year after the end of the Second World War, Italy became a republic and the monarchy was rejected. In the midst of the ruins of war groups of protestors began to form and agitate in defence of women, crying out for secular education for preschool children. They were demanding the recognition of the the national, political, cultural and economic significance of the role of motherhood and of the rights of children.

Malaguzzi's own narrative of how the Reggio Emilia preschools began.

In March 1992 I was very fortunate to be able to visit Emilia Romagna as part of a group interested in learning more about what was happening in the preschools, which were just then becoming famous. During the visit we met Loris Malaguzzi. In fact, we spent an afternoon listening to him talking about how the whole wonderful process had started. This is the story he told us, transposed from the notes I took at the time:

> The people in this region suffered badly during the war and after the war there was despair but also hope. Houses were being rebuilt and we all felt something like power, because now we had the chance to take control of our lives and build a better future. We thought particularly hard about the children. They had suffered so much for so long. And it was against this backdrop that the story I am going to tell you was set.
>
> A group of peasant women, up in the hills in the town of Villa Cella, which is only about seven kilometres from Reggio, came upon an abandoned German tank, a truck and horses. These things were precious beyond belief at that time. And, as I have already said, the people were hungry and poor. They quickly recognised that what they had found gave them some resources and the power to make changes to their lives and communities. They salvaged some bricks and sold them together with the truck, tank and horses for 800,000 lire. The money went to the Committee of National Liberation (the CNL) and it was agreed – after much debate and discussion – that the money should go to building a school. Interestingly the men had wanted to build a theatre and that is something worth thinking about, but the women were determined that the money be spent on a preschool. Can you see how important culture was and still is – culture in the sense of recording and preserving what we, as a group, have made and value and which can be built on to enhance our lives?
>
> The villagers were fierce in their determination to provide some education for young children that was not under the control of the Catholic Church, which had been supportive of fascism during the war. They wanted a new form of education which would ensure that they would never again bring up generations of children who would be subject to injustice and inequality. A local farmer donated some land and people from all around – workers and peasants – some of them the parents of young children and some not – worked at night and weekends to build the school. A local building cooperative also offered its services as well as the use of some machinery. (Personal notes)

Malaguzzi also recorded his feelings in his personal writing. Here is what he said after his first visit to see the beginning of the building of the first school in Villa Cella:

> I went home. My feelings of wonder, and the sense of the extraordinary, were stronger than my happiness. … All of my little models were

laughingly overturned; that building a school would ever occur to the people, women, farm labourers, factory workers, farmers was in itself traumatic. But that these same people, without a penny to their names, with no technical offices, building permits, site directors, inspectors from the Ministry of Education or the Party, could actually build a school with their own strength, brick by brick, was the second paradox.
(Malaguzzi 2000:13, cited in Thornton and Brunton 2005: 10)

Building had started on 1 May 1945 and, after eight months of hard work, intense community involvement and participation, the school was opened by the mayor and admitted its first 30 students. It was named *The April 25th School* in honour of liberation day, and the plaque on the face of the building bears a moving and inspirational inscription:

Men and women working together, we built the walls of this school because we wanted a new and different place for our children. May 1945

An example had been set and a powerful statement made about what was possible in order to get what was being seen as essential – a decent future for the children of the region. Men and women, with intact ideals, had taken charge of their own lives and changed history. They had fought for children's legitimate rights and life chances based on the essential principle of taking children seriously. It is interesting to note that taking children and their rights seriously was not new. Another preschool had been set up in nearby by Sesso and named *Martiri di Sesso* (the Martyrs of Sesso) in memory of the 33 people executed there by the fascists between 1943 and 1945. The movement spread and it is worth noting the vital role played by women in leading it.
   Malaguzzi himself continued telling us his story.

When I heard about the school in Villa Cella I was a teacher in the early stages of my career and heard that peasant women were building a school so I jumped on my bicycle to go and have a look. I saw women clearing bricks near the river and when I asked what they were doing they told me they were building a school. I told them I was a teacher and they asked if I would look after their children. What they said to me I will never forget: 'Our children are as intelligent as rich people's children and we want someone to teach them to give them a better chance in life.' I told them that I had no experience but promised I would do what I could. I told them that I would learn with them as we went along.
(Personal notes)

For Malaguzzi, this was a formative experience. He was only 25 years old but he learned what proved to be an ongoing lesson: that history can, indeed, be changed, and the most likely way to make this happen is through liberating and high-quality education, which is delivered to the children and involves parents and the community.

Over the coming years Malaguzzi, learning on the hoof, decided it was essential to engage as widely as possible with the community of Reggio Emilia, in order to explain his aims and goals and to win their trust and respect. He told us of some amazing trips taken to visit the isolated villages in the high mountains:

> We managed to persuade the railways to lend us a train – just for one day. We packed the train full of lovely and exciting things – puppets, paints and paper. And we decorated the train on the outside to make it look magical. At each little village we would set up a stall in the piazza or in more remote places lay a trail of exciting things – like paper footsteps on the ground or flying paper birds in the trees – to entice the children to bring their parents out to find us. Then we would tell the parents what we wanted to do whilst the children played and danced and painted. (Personal notes)

In a DVD made by *Reggio Children* and tracing the magical story of the birth of the preschools, there are some wonderful scenes of the many whole-day events organised regularly there and in other towns to explain and show people the work being done by the children and their teachers. We see children painting wonderful pictures, dancing in the streets, dressing up and acting out their own stories and more.

In the late 1950s, when the economy in Italy began to boom, people migrated to the north, and to the large urban centres, away from the countryside and the poorer south. Women with young children entered the labour market in greater numbers. It is not surprising, then, that it was during this period that, in response to the demands of parents, the municipality of Reggio Emilia began to set up preschools for children aged 3 to 6. What was most significant was that these were secular schools, free from church control. It was at this time that the municipality also took over control of the original *scuole dell'infanzia*, first been set up in 1945. It is deeply moving to know that, up until this point, the original scuole dell'infanzia had been entirely managed by teams of people drawn from the local communities – parents, trades unions, workers, teachers and other stakeholders. In 1970 the first *nidi* (infant-toddler centres), catering for children from 3 months to 3 years old, was opened by the municipality in response to requests from working mothers.

Malaguzzi, doing and learning by doing, had become the key educational expert and planner for the children in the scuole dell'infanzia (and later for the nidi and for today's combined centres) and presided over the transfer from local control to the control of the municipality. This was not a period free from stress, tension or political opposition, but through continuing debate, the exercise of diplomacy and respect for the views of all, developments continued.

Some influences on Malaguzzi's thinking.

We know little about what Malaguzzi read or studied and relatively little of his writing survives from his early adult years. We know that he encountered the thoughts and ideas of *John Dewey*, the eminent American thinker who saw children as an oppressed group, lacking a voice and always subject to the control of adults. Motivated to improve the lives of the less fortunate in society, he began to think about how best to educate children living in tenements, on crowded city streets or farms or having migrated from one country to another. He was concerned with things like social class, poverty, prejudice, rights and wrongs. He wanted to reform the schooling system so that it related more clearly to the social changes that took place during and after the war. For Dewey, each child was an individual who, in the new America, no longer played a vital role within the family or home or the world of work. Dewey himself was a remarkable thinker and his work continues to influence many aspects of educational provision not only in America but more widely. He insisted that schools should be open to all children, who should actively participate with the help and guidance of teachers. Children would learn to behave cooperatively and they would change society accordingly. These were ideas that spoke to Malaguzzi's growing awareness.

It is almost certain that Malaguzzi knew intimately the philosophical and political work of *Antonio Gramsci*, which involved appreciating the importance of power relationships, equity and injustice in providing educational opportunities for children and their families. Gramsci developed, among other concepts, the idea of 'cultural hegemony' as the way to challenge capitalism, and its effect particularly on developed Western culture. According to him, trying to displace those holding power through brute force does not work. What is required is that those wishing to challenge the status quo must gradually work to criticise and change the prevailing norms and values. This applies, as you will realise, particularly to the education of the young. Remember that Malaguzzi wanted the children being educated in his preschools to be able to question the existing structures and values, the power base of the Catholic Church, which had supported fascism, and an existing culture of women having few, if any, rights. By thinking about and questioning such things they would be in a position to challenge and change.

For Gramsci, this change needed to be accomplished on many fronts and especially in education. For this to happen, public education via the national school system must move to teach, at the most fundamental levels, new ways of thinking and doing. This gave Malaguzzi fuel for his plans to ensure the ongoing support of local government in being part of the revolutionary changes he was proposing. What was in place before the changes was the system of 'banking education', with passive learners being educated to fill particular roles in society and provided with knowledge by the more expert adults. Malaguzzi was thinking about something more organic, challenging and potentially threatening, unless those holding at least some of the power – and the money – were brought on board.

Gramsci's writing is complex and written in dense language, often difficult to unpick. What Malaguzzi took from his ideas is the belief that even the weakest and poorest in society can gain power to challenge existing norms and practices when they work together towards a common social goal. Together they can overturn accepted practices that appear unjust and unfair. Think about how women achieved the vote in the United Kingdom by working together to challenge the status quo, in order to improve the lot of their fellow women. Now think about the peasant women in Reggio Emilia and what they did to challenge the status quo there, in order to improve the lot of children and working mothers.

We know that Malaguzzi read and was influenced by the work of both *Jean Piaget* and *Lev Vygotsky*. In his writing and his speech he referred to them as *our* Piaget and *our* Vygotsky. The use of this possessive pronoun is understandable and even moving with regard to Vygotsky, who Malaguzzi admired throughout his life, but referring to Piaget in a similarly inclusive way is intriguing, since Malaguzzi's views became so different from those of Piaget. Rinaldi's explanation is that the intimate voice implied by the use of 'our' reflected his feelings of gratitude for the guidance Piaget offered him in his early years as a teacher. When he later started to be more aware of the importance of dialogue with the children he began to question Piaget's lack of emphasis on the historical, social and cultural. *Our* Vygotsky and *our* Malaguzzi came from systems that denied opportunities to groups of people and restricted opportunities for others. It is not in the least surprising that Malaguzzi was determined that any analysis of a system – be it education, health care or housing – had to be in light of history, in light of the past. So, when planning to offer a new system of preschool education for the children in Reggio Emilia, Malaguzzi took detailed and careful account of the past. He was determined that young learners should ask their own questions and seek their own answers, supported by interested and appropriately educated adults.

Vygotsky's view of learning was that it was essentially social so, although he, like Piaget, saw the infant learner as a tireless explorer, he set this tireless explorer in a context and a culture, within which there were others, some of whom were more expert than the little explorer and could therefore both model and support her learning. Vygotsky wrote a great deal about the learner's potential being different from what the learner was seen or heard to be able to do, and talked of the zone of proximal development (ZPD), where the learner can be assisted to move from observed achievement to a higher level.

I do not know whether or not Malaguzzi encountered the work of *Paolo Freire*, but I do know that they would have shared many ideas and principles and that there is a school in Reggio Emilia named after him. Both worked for a democratic education: Freire working in his native Brazil for the vast cohorts of illiterate adults, trying to enable them to be able to read and to question their world, whilst Malaguzzi was working with children and their families to enable the very youngest children not only to answer questions, but to raise them. Both saw the significance of what we often call *dialogic education*, where the learner is not the passive empty vessel to be filled, but the active seeker of meaning. Freire had been influenced by Dewey and Vygotsky, and can be called a social constructivist, much like Malaguzzi. They would have had many points of contact.

Malaguzzi had followed what *Maria Montessori* was saying and doing. As the first female physician in Italy, she reflected what we might call a late nineteenth-century version of European progressive philosophical thinking, following in the footsteps of such eminent philosophers as *Rousseau, Pestalozzi* and *Seguin*. She believed that all children had what she called 'natural intelligence', which she defined as being rational, empirical and spiritual. She fell foul of the fascists and fled the country to go to the United States, where, for a time, her approach flourished.

Later in his life Malaguzzi encountered the work of *Uri Bronfenbrenner*, which looked in detail at culture, context and society, talking about the layers of environment, each of which has an effect on any child, from the most intimate setting of the home (which he called the *microsystem*); up through the *mesosystem*, where the child encounters and makes connections with teachers, religious leaders, neighbours and so on; on to the *exosystem*, which is remote physically from the child but impacts on her – the rules of the parents workplace, community based resources and so on; to the most remote setting of the *macrosystem*, which is made up the cultural values, customs and laws that apply to the child and her family. Some talk also of the *chronosystem*, which relates to the timing of events – like the effect on the child when a parent dies, or someone has a birthday or moves to a new school or a new house, or enters the next class. We will examine the impact of some of this on Malaguzzi's thinking.

He read the writings of *Jerome Bruner*, met him, talked to him and came to regard him as a friend. This great American psychologist, writer and thinker had been born blind and is still alive and active today. When you visit Reggio Children and the Malaguzzi Centre you will find photographs of and messages from Bruner, alongside similar photographs and messages from people like Nelson Mandela. During his early years as a researcher, Bruner's passion had been early learning and he shared many of Vygotsky's ideas: he believed that all learning was social, that language was essential to learning, that culture and context are defining features, that more expert others can support and scaffold learning, that meaning making and sharing come about primarily through narrative, that games and rituals in are vital in early learning and much, much more.

The last influence I will mention is *Howard Gardner*, not because he is the most or least significant, but because my list must end somewhere. Gardner is best known for his work around multiple intelligences. He believed that intelligence could not be defined as any single entity or measured in any meaningful way. He has challenged much of Piaget's work and is a firm believer in individuality, creativity and that we live in an imperfect world. He was born in Pennsylvania to parents who had fled from Germany in 1938 with their 3-year-old son Eric, who was killed in a sleighing accident just before Howard's birth. No one discussed the flight from Germany or the death of his sibling with him, but he became aware that, in his family, physical risks were not taken and there was a strong focus on intellectual and creative pursuits. He was a successful student and eventually went to Harvard College, where he encountered *Erikson*, the psychoanalyst, *Riesman*, the sociologist, and our friend Jerome Bruner, with whom he later worked. Do read his work if you are interested in it. Essentially, he initially identified seven intelligences. These were linguistic, logico-mathematical, musical, bodily-kinesthetic, spatial, interpersonal and intrapersonal. He later extended the list to include naturalist, spiritual, moral and existential intelligence. When we come to look at Malaguzzi's ideas we will find the influence of Gardner's work in many of them.

The political otherness of Reggio

In their introduction to Rinaldi's seminal book on Reggio Emilia, *Gunilla Dahlberg* and *Peter Moss*, outline very clearly just what it was in the political history and culture of Reggio Emilia that allowed what happened to occur. They start with a reminder that the events in Reggio Emilia could be seen as a pedagogical experiment involving a whole community. This experiment has now been ongoing for more than 45 years, which makes it something quite unique. Nothing like it has taken place anywhere in the world, not even in America, where, Gardner reminds us, they pride themselves on promoting cooperative learning, creativity in the curriculum, parental involvement, community participation on paper, the discovery method and more – but all on adult terms. We could say the same of what happens here in the UK. Much is said about valuing creativity, fostering curiosity and independence, inclusion, diversity, the importance of parental support and so on, and yet we continue to test children from almost the minute they cross the threshold into formal educational settings. Much of what makes Reggio so special is the willingness – no, the urgency – of being both questioning and critical of what they do, and the realisation that, for a pedagogical experiment to work, it needs to be understood, valued and respected by all those it touches. These are the children, of course, and their parents, but also those who work in the schools, encounter the children, have been children and will be children. It is an essential embedded feature of the community.

The staff in Reggio have continued to bring in new ideas from various disciplines and across cultures. Malaguzzi was a firm believer in the fact that education or pedagogy cannot not be seen as an isolated discipline. It is deeply rooted in society with its values, norms, beliefs, practices and changes. This makes it political in essence and having to respond to changes in economy, sciences, arts, human relations or customs. Each of these affects all children – even the youngest children – who, living in a social world, make sense of what they see or hear in order to read the word and deal with its realities. For Malaguzzi, the ideas he and his colleagues held could be compared to a tangle of spaghetti, suggesting that learning does not move in a logical, sequenced fashion but through starts and stops, jumps, leaps and retreats. This is an important feature of the work in Reggio and something that, like all else, is rooted in its particular history.

But what makes Reggio so 'other' for me and for many others is its implicit belief in the possibility of creating systems that are democratic and radical. This arises from the history and culture of Reggio itself. We have seen something of how early childhood services in Reggio were built on a long tradition of collective life in communities bonded together by common needs and practices, building reciprocity and trust. Putnam (1993) talked of this as *social capital*. Here (and elsewhere) in Italy was fertile soil for the growth of left politics. But there is more. The story of Reggio is essentially also the story of women and their struggle to improve not only their own lives and rights, but the rights of children. These rights lie at the heart of this story of the struggle against fascism, injustice and monopoly.

Another possibly unique aspect of the Reggio system was the long-term engagement in the development of financial and other support for the preschool system given by successive mayors and municipalities. Luigi Roversi, mayor between 1902 and 1920, socialist and humanitarian, oversaw the opening in 1912 of a secular nursery school, the *Villa Gaia*. He wanted to create and support a school where education was going to be a tool against poverty, ignorance and fear. In short, a tool for freedom to think, to question and to contribute. What do you think one of the first actions of the fascist governor in the early 1920s was? It was to close the school.

We have seen how, at the end of the Second World War, women were becoming more vocal and active in their demand for a place of learning in which to leave their children when they went out to work, which was not only a public, but also a quality, place. It was the women who stated that quality was an essential ingredient. In 1945 they formed the Union of Italian Women (*Unione Donne Italiane*, or UDI) to work for the rights of women from many groups in society, who had expressed their willingness to work together for their emancipation. At that time women did not have the right to vote, to maternity leave or to equity in the job market. The UDI was a national organisation but worked also at a regional and local level. It was at this level in Reggio that the organisation was so successful in enabling women to become serious, active protagonists in civil society. At the end of the war there was a Communist Party majority in Reggio and, through their support and that of many citizens, the vital role of the municipality developed.

This meant that there was support throughout the years: along with this came some funding; the development of negotiated and agreed terms of employment and education for the workers; community and trades union involvement; engagement with women's groups and consultation on pedagogy. As an example, Malaguzzi insisted on discussing and debating his proposal that each nido and scuola dell'infanzia should be equipped with a studio (or *atelier*), where a teacher/artist/scientist could engage in their own work. It was his belief that children having open access to such a workspace and artist would benefit enormously. You have only to look at the work that emerged over the years to see how right he was. But he needed those with a stake in the system – the parents, teachers, workers and children, and those providing for them, to have a say in questioning and deciding the wisdom of his proposal. You will know that the atelier became a defining feature of all the preschool provision.

Between 1971 and 1972, Malaguzzi, together with parents, the municipality, the unions and the women's groups, worked towards new legislation (which appeared in 1973) for the scuole dell'infanzia and nidi. As a result, men were employed in the preschools, all teachers had to have a high school diploma or a degree, and the working week was set at 36 hours to include dedicated time for professional development and in-service training. There were to be two teachers and a helper to each class, an *atelierista*, a cook and a pedagogista (organiser and coordinator) to liaise with the feeder nidi and the receiving schools. Each centre was to set up a school council, where pedagogical and didactic issues were debated. Now, although there are still some nidi and scuole dell'infanzia, there is a growing move for these two types of provision to work together.

In 1978 Gustavo Selva, a national radio commentator, launched a very nasty seven-day offensive against the policies of the municipality with regard to their early childhood provision. This was dealt with in the most democratic and transparent way possible. Malaguzzi and his colleagues, together with the municipality, opened up the scuole dell'infanzie and the nidi to both public scrutiny and community debate over a period of several months. They chose not to run from criticism but to take it seriously and address each issue that arose. This was a positive, time-consuming and essentially democratic way of dealing with it. We return to the ideas around early childhood education and democracy in Chapter 9.

Looking back, looking ahead

In this opening chapter we have looked at the little we know about the personal life of a very private person, but, importantly, examined closely the context within which he developed his ideas; the history of where he was born, grew up, was educated and lived; the significant events in his working life and the people whose work influenced his thinking. He was an educator, someone for whom pedagogy (the art and science of teaching) was to do with much more than the simple transmission of knowledge. It was through his sensitive and acute observations of children, as he stood alongside them, looking and listening to them, that he noted the very pleasure they took in the processes of learning, knowing and understanding, For him, this was an indication that these feelings of joy and sometimes triumph must be fostered in order that the pleasure of learning and of knowing, of making and sharing meaning, of expressing feelings, of asking and answering questions would survive, despite the difficulties and effort sometimes required.

In the chapters that follow we will chart his ideas on pedagogy in some detail, but all the while you are urged to remember that what happened in Reggio Emilia could only have happened in Reggio Emilia. Some educators, moved to tears by the beauty of the children's art work, the sight of the wonderful buildings and the moving tributes made to Reggio, believe that they can adopt the approach for themselves. There is much to learn from Reggio, but it is vital to recall that it is not a recipe or a curriculum, or something that can simply be adapted from one place, one culture, one history to another.

Glossary of unfamiliar terms

In *Introducing Vygotsky* a glossary followed each chapter; in *Introducing Bruner* it was felt one glossary at the end of the book would be more straight-forward and that is what you will find in this book. So if you come to a word – in English, Italian or any other language – whose meaning is not clear, do turn to the glossary for help.

Chapter 2

What makes Reggio Emilia so special?

> Stand aside for a while and leave room for learning, observe carefully what children do, and then, if you have understood well, perhaps teaching will be different from before.
>
> (Malaguzzi in Edwards *et al.* 2011: 57)

The Reggio Emilia preschools have no predetermined curriculum; they carry out no tests on the children nor do they have to meet goals or targets. The teachers are not required to hold any undergraduate qualifications. And yet they are often described as offering the best provision for young children in the world. How has this come about?

Theory and practice

Malaguzzi read widely and was influenced by many of the theorists who contributed to the thinking of many Western countries – Bruner, Vygotsky, Piaget, Bronfennbrenner and Dewey, but also other theorists, some of whom are little known or not highly regarded here.

He was influenced by the philosophers *Frances and David Hawkins*, both of whom visited Reggio at least twice and worked abroad in many developed and developing countries. They were interested in children as competent and curious beings and in the importance of children being able to follow their own interests. David Hawkins drew a distinction between being able to mess about and making a mess. The important difference is that of intention. Children messing about actively and consciously engage in explorations and investigations; the teacher's role is then to closely observe, document, revisit, and interpret the work of the children, together with families, colleagues and the children themselves. You can see how close this is to what developed in Reggio Emilia.

David Hawkins described a project that he and his partner set up and what they, the adults, learned about children as the children 'messed about'. The project related to things that roll, and how and why:

As a faculty, we were seeking to better support the children's interest in rolling through our own investigations. We filled the room's shelves with recycled materials, adhesives, wire, ropes, measuring tapes, wood pieces, and cardboard, and we began to create cars. After building and field-testing many cars, we invited a small group of children to comment on our work. The children wondered why we built cars, many of which did not roll very far or very fast and others that did not roll at all. In their work, parallel to ours, the children were categorizing objects by their ability to roll fast and far, referred to by the children as 'rollability'. While the teachers were immediately immersed in the theme of transportation, the children taught us that the work was about the concepts inherent in rolling, such as velocity, acceleration, distance, time, and friction. The initial work on rolling has led to schoolwide investigations of incline, both existing and constructed, and of a related concept, chain reaction.

(Kluger-Bell, cited in Hall 2010)

Also influential was the work of *Serge Moscovici*, who looked at what was necessary for people, including small children, to be able to talk to one another in groups. He believed that they must have a system of shared understanding, in particular of concepts and ideas that are outside of 'common' understanding or that have particular meaning for that group. He called this *social representation*, where words become imbued with special meanings within particular social groups. In the example given by David Hawkins we can see how the group of children invited to join the science experiment in their classroom invented and adopted the word 'rollability'. We are all familiar with the language of lawyers, which is so impenetrable to outsiders, and increasingly to the languages of Twitter and other social media systems, which are impenetrable to those not part of this culture. So social representation can be defined as:

Systems of values, ideas and practices with a two-fold function; first, to establish an order which will enable individuals to orientate themselves in their material and social world and to master it; secondly, to enable communication to take place amongst members of a community by providing them with a code for social exchange and a code for naming and classifying unambiguously the various aspects of their world and their individual and group history.

(Moscovici 1973)

What is particularly significant about this is that meaning is created through a system of social negotiations rather than being a fixed and defined thing, and that its interpretation may well require an understanding of additional aspects of that social environment. When you come to read the chapter about the making of the theatre curtain you will find some examples of the language the children appropriated for themselves – words like transformation and cell – where the words have become part of their vocabularies sometimes because one child has introduced a new word into the group (like cell) and sometimes because the word usage has arisen through interaction with an adult (like transformation)

Another person whose work influenced Malaguzzi was the Swiss psychologist *Gabriel Mugny*, who looked at the performance of individuals alone or in groups and found that performance was better in the latter, but only where there was an element of conflict. This is an interesting and potentially disturbing finding. However, on careful reading, it emerges that conflict in this instance means two or more individuals within a group disagreeing about exactly how to do something and having to resolve this conflict in some way. This can be said to be a cognitive conflict or a socio-cognitive conflict. Malaguzzi talks of Mugny's finding as *interpersonal cognitive constructions*.

Let us examine an example that shows how very young children, working collaboratively, can demonstrate disagreement (or have cognitive conflict) and learn from it:

> Two groups of children – one of boys and the other of girls – have been working on a design for the curtain to be put in the theatre in Reggio Emilia. At the end of a long process only one design can be chosen and the children have to decide which. They argue for a long time, with the boys all agreeing that theirs is the best, whilst the girls fiercely defend theirs. When no conclusion is reached Leonardo suggests that they should let all the children in the class vote, but Giovanni says that this will not help because all the boys will vote for the boy's design and the girls for the girl's design. Finally Federica says, 'I'm about to change my mind. Let's do this: let's decide for theirs, let's vote for theirs.'
>
> (Drawn on Vecchi 2002: 90–91)

It is interesting that Malaguzzi was also influenced by the English educationalist *Wilfred Carr*'s ideas on the relationship between theory and practice. Carr turned his critical eye on the work of the so-called *reflective practitioner* and action research approaches that became popular during the late 1980s, as there was growing dissatisfaction with older and more traditional teaching approaches. These new approaches insisted on practice rather than theory. Carr was interested in exploring the idea that teaching, an essentially practical activity, had to start with theory, but argued that this was not necessarily the case. Malaguzzi took from this that too-early and too-heavy reliance on theory could damage the creativity and spontaneity that is possible where teachers trust their observations and instincts and use theory and their own experience to confirm. For him, the teacher became the researcher, the maker of theory.

Research

For Malaguzzi, the business of teachers and learners was to learn and re-learn together. In this way children are not shaped by experience, but shape it themselves. He believed that children's learning could be looked at in two ways. The first is the way they come into an activity and develop their own strategies and ways of thinking and taking action. The second is the way in which objects are transformed. I could not find examples to illustrate this, but here is a little vignette that seems to show young children exploring art and science in one tiny exchange.

Two 6-year-old girls come into the nursery where a piece of translucent white paper has been pasted onto the glass. The adult did this, having noticed the leaves casting shadows. So she did something in response to what she had noticed about the physical world and presumably to offer another way of looking at it.

This is how the discussion between the two girls went:

AGNESE   It is a drawing made by little bits of sun.
CECILIA   They seem to be tiny leaves of sun.
AGNESE   It is the shadow of the leaves that is reflected.
CECILIA   But is it a drawing by the sun or by the shadow?
AGNESE   It is like a clock. I saw it also yesterday and the other day. When that drawing comes up [pointing to the signs on the translucent paper] it is time to go to lunch.

(Gandini in Edwards *et al.* 2011: 306)

It is a wonderful example of children looking, asking questions, making hypotheses, listening to one other and exploring art and science. But I am not sure if this is children coming into an activity or transforming objects. I think it is children raising questions, sharing ideas and discovering something about the physical world.

It may be true that adults and children learn differently and use different procedures, abide by different rules, develop different hypotheses and theories and follow different paths. If you go back to the 'rollability' project you will see something of these aspects.

The purpose of the research that teachers do, either on their own or with colleagues, is to develop and use strategies that will be useful to children's learning. They go from research into action or from action into research. It becomes a spiral process. You will find reference to the research that teachers have undertaken all the time, every day in their lives in the preschools, throughout this book. It is the very stuff of their working lives.

The effects of this are numerous. Teachers learn that they cannot expect or ask children to give back to them what they already know: they – the teachers – are always learning. Children come to be better known by their teachers.

This gives the children confidence to work with peers in unusual and some-times difficult situations. They become more persistent in following their goals. They become able to make more and wider choices.

The preschools are set up so as to allow children the utmost flexibility in making choices. They can find places to be alone, or with a small group, or with a bigger group, with or without teachers, in the atelier, the mini atelier or the large piazza, or outside in good weather. Each classroom is then a large space full of what Malaguzzi called 'market stalls', each offering children a choice of their own projects or activities. Malaguzzi believes this way of setting up the space reflects the city in which they live, with its squares and porticoes and its gracious central square that sometimes becomes a real buzzing market. According to Bruner, this market acts in the same way as a what he called a forum:

> A culture is as much a forum for negotiating and renegotiating meaning and for explicating action as it is a set of rules or specifications for action. … It is the forum aspect of a culture that gives its participants a role in constantly making and remaking the culture – an active role as partici-pants rather than as a performing spectators who play out their canonical roles according to rule when the appropriate cue occurs.
>
> (Bruner 1986: 123)

What is more, there is no planned curriculum and this, says Malaguzzi, is because that would push the schools towards teaching without learning. So the curriculum becomes a series of long-term and shorter projects. These may be planned by the teachers, but the ways in which the children respond is up to them. A project on designing a curtain for the theatre might become a project about transformation for one group of children, about cells for another, or about upside-down domes for a third. It is important to remember that in each school year the children build on what they have done before and, Malaguzzi believes, their experience gives them standing in the school community, so they are taken seriously, which enables the teachers to follow the children. He likes the word 'reconnaissance' and applies it to describing how the teachers use their experience in their meetings and discussions, exhibitions and workshops with colleagues, political figures, community members, children, advisory bodies, family members, visitors and others.

Let us look now at the roles of two pedagogical specialists within the system: the pedagogista and the atelierista. The role of pedagogista or peda-gogical coordinator started in centres like Bologna, Modena, Parma and Pistoia in the mid-1970s, when a few municipalities began to open their own preschools. The role is deeply embedded in the Reggio system and the pedagogisti work on a collegiate basis, with their own group of scuole and nidi, but also in interactions with other working groups. At present (2012) there are 13 pedagogisti, 10 of whom coordinate the municipal provision and each of whom work directly and intimately with four schools or centres. The other two have wider and more senior positions relating to the pedagogical work across the city.

The work of the pedagogisti is, in some ways, like that of advisory teachers in the UK. At the heart of their work is professional development and this, as you know, is an essential element of all teachers' work and delivered on a weekly basis. The pedagogisti are concerned to ensure that this can be offered in ways that are respectful of individual needs and preferences in terms of time and modality. So they attempt to arrange meetings that may be separate and specialist, but also joint. The pedagogisti say that, as professionals, they aim to use theory to back up practice and, since their work is very complex, they are in regular and constant contact with a range of stakeholders. When explaining something to a group of parents, for example, pedagogisti may need to be able to offer pedagogical reasons, together with political and budgetary constraints, in explanation. They are very much encouraged in their roles by the ongoing support of mayors over three generations of children.

The word atelierista is sometimes translated as studio teacher, but in essence the ateliersta is something for which there is no English equivalent. The atelier, a French word for studio, is a workshop or laboratory at the heart of every preschool and in that atelier is someone called the atelierista.

The atelier was established from the very start of the project, in 1963, at first in every scuola dell'infanzia that was built and later into every *asilo nido* as well. The presence of this dedicated space, together with the framework of learning and teaching strategies, was a deliberate retort to the marginal role that was, until then, assigned to expressive education. More than that, it was a reaction against the accepted forms of educating young children based on words and simple routines. Children were now regarded as competent, curious, questioning, creative and logical. This child – the new child – was entitled to a school made up of respect, relationships, listening and learning. Teachers, too, were entitled to a school made up of respect: relationships, teaching and learning. The atelier became a particular space, in Malaguzzi's words:

> a space for digging with one's own hands and one's own mind, for refining one's own eyes, through the practice of the visual arts. It had to be a place for sensitizing one's taste and aesthetic sense, a place for the individual exploration of projects connected with experiences planned in the different classrooms of the school ... a place for researching motivations and theories of children from scribbles on up, a place for exploring variations in tools, techniques and materials with which to work ...
>
> (Edwards *et al.* 2005: 7)

The atelier was then going to be a place of challenge and provocation. And for Malaguzzi, although his great plans were not fully realised, the atelier did not disappoint. It was the place where children could use all their expressive languages and, as it happened, their mathematical, scientific and logical ones as well. It was, and still is, a place for research.

After his death, the old Locatelli Parmesan cheese storage facility was turned into the Loris Malaguzzi International Centre. Within it is a large atelier and, since 2006, this has hosted the *Raggio di Luce* or Ray of Light, a place for research, experimentation and immersion in an environment where light, in its various forms, can be investigated by means of explorations that provoke curiosity and wonder, and stimulate creativity and in-depth study. It is also a place of research related to science. Designed for both individuals and groups, there are specifically devised contexts, instruments and tools, all designed to make the exploration of light more apparent and spectacular. I visited it some years ago, sadly on a day when I was the only visitor in the centre, but the young atelierista, who had managed to get through the snow to work, showed me all the wonderful equipment together with the comments, questions and artwork of the children. Here again was evidence of children's abilities to take hold of a topic and pursue it in individual and different ways to come to some understanding.

In the first few years atelieristi were only to be found in the scuole dell'infanzia primarily for financial reasons, but also because there was a belief that the role needed to be redefined. Now, as there are more and more combined centres providing for children from birth to the age of 6, atelieristi are employed in them and in wider settings. These include the Documentation and Educational Research Centre, which was established to be a resource for highlighting and formally recognising the experience of the municipal infant-toddler centres and preschools, and of the local educational institutions in general. It provides opportunities for exchange and professional enrichment by promoting and supporting the now-accepted culture of documentation and educational research as an *integral part* of the professionalism of educators. The centre also collaborates with Reggio Children on the creation and management of exhibitions related to projects designed and carried out by the infant-toddler centres and preschools operated by the municipality of Reggio Emilia, as well as other schools on the local territory. The Gianni Rodari Theatre Laboratory and the Video Centre work in close collaboration with the Documentation Centre.

The role of the atelierista is complex and important, and Vea Vecchi has written an excellent book on the subject. At present, the role of the atelierista is seen to be that of providing a rich and invitingly open-to-questioning environment for the children, but also to be a researcher into both children's and adult's ways of knowing. Vecchi ascribes an additional role: that of providing not only the tools and techniques, but also the specific language and vocabulary involved in the creative arts. More of that is to be found in the *Raggio di Luce*, where the language being offered is scientific.

Looking back, looking ahead

In this chapter we have looked at Malaguzzi's thinking about the relationship between theory and practice, and have seen how he became convinced that theory without practice was empty and that all those working with children had to become active researchers. Research must be a joint process between the learners and the educators exploring and learning together. Collaboration, negotiation, respect, listening, sharing and relationships are all key to this joint process and it was enormously aided by the introduction of the studio/workshop, and later the laboratory in the provision.

In the next chapter we turn our attention to the importance of relationships to all learning. Malaguzzi's socio-cultural model could not exist in a world where children are seen as isolated individuals. They come, as he said, with pieces of the world attached.

Chapter 3

The importance of relationships

> Among the goals of our approach is to reinforce each child's sense of identity through a recognition that comes from peers and adults, so much so that each one would feel enough sense of belonging and self-confidence to participate in the activities of the school. In this way, we promote in children the widening of communication networks and mastery and appreciation of language in all its levels and contextual uses.
>
> (Malaguzzi in Edwards *et al.* 2011: 45)

In his writing Malaguzzi talked at length about what he called a 'pedagogy of relationships'. This is at the heart of all the work done in Reggio Emilia. In this chapter we examine what he meant by this, how it operates in practice and why it matters

The child

We often say 'the child must come first', or 'we think about the interests of the child'. For Malaguzzi, there was no such thing as 'the child'. 'The child' is too abstract for him, too removed from what makes each individual child – and adult – unique. For him, each child arrives with what he called 'pieces of the world attached'. The child who arrives in the scuola dell'infanzia or nido already has relationships with parents or carers, grandparents, siblings, aunts and uncles, cousins, neighbours, friends and peers, the staff at the local clinic, the people who work in the local shops and more: a network of tight and loose connections that will expand and contract throughout the child's life. This network of relationships has implications for what must happen in educational settings.

Traditionally, when you think about what happens in a school or other educational situation, you almost certainly think about the dyad – the pair or duo – of the child and the teacher. In thinking of a pedagogy of relationships, Malaguzzi, as you would expect, adopts a much more sociohistorical and sociocultural approach, and thinks of the triad (or threesome) of the child, the teacher and the family (or, by implication the wider triadic relationships of the children, the teachers and members of the child's immediate and extended family).

We have touched on the extremely significant roles played in the development of the Reggio preschools by women agitating for their and their children's rights, and of people in the local community becoming involved in the construction, maintenance and even governance of the preschools. We have also considered how the municipality supported the developments of the preschool system both philosophically and financially, and read about community members being drawn into the everyday life of the preschools through events in their villages and town, and through getting involved in the discussions about teaching and learning over decades.

In light of this, it is not surprising that, for Malaguzzi, the idea of being primarily concerned with the simple dyad would mean accepting an artificial world, remote from the reality of the child's more complex, nuanced everyday world full of the close and less-close relationships described earlier.

Perhaps you now accept that it is not possible to think of the child – any child – in the abstract. Let me now ask you to think of a child – an individual child, perhaps your own child or another child with whom you have a particular link. That child – whoever you think about – is already connected and linked to her own reality and it is this that must be accepted, reflected and valued.

The children described below are all in the reception class at the same school and are drawn from the same community. Here are pen portraits of some of the children, submitted by a student on an early childhood studies programme:

> Mary Jane is the youngest of nine children. They live in a large house which has a small garden at the back. She shares a bed with her sister in a room with all the other girls in the family. The boys have their own room and mum and dad another room. An aunt also lives with them and she lives in the room at the very top of the house. They are very friendly with the people who live in the house next door and all attend church every Sunday morning.

> Bilaal is an only child. His dad is a journalist and his mother is a teacher. They live in a small house and he has his own bedroom but there is no garden. He doesn't have any friends on his street but plays with the children in the nursery and is just making friends with two children who live not far away.

> Arnie and Rosa are twins who live with their mum in a flat on a large estate. Their mum works in the local library and the children love going there as often as they can to look at the books. The other people who

work at the library know the children very well and since they have children too all the children often play together. They go to different schools. They do not attend any church or mosque or synagogue.

Zeynep lives with her mum and dad and grandparents above her dad's dry cleaning shop. They are very integrated into the local Turkish community and often visit one another's houses, attend parties and weddings and enjoy listening to Turkish music.

Joseph is the second son of Isiah and Ruth. The family live in a two up two down modernised house which has a small garden in front and a larger garden behind. This is a Jewish family and the two boys go to Hebrew classes. The father is a lawyer and the mother works in the home.

Zena lives with her two mums in the house next door to the house of Isiah and Ruth. One of her mum's is a dinner lady and the other is training to become a social worker. Zena goes to the after-school club every day where she is making new friends.

It is very apparent even from these tiny biographies that each of these children is a unique individual, with a complicated network of relationships with family members or others in their immediate communities. Would you think that they are always perceived and treated as unique individuals at their school? The student who made these notes overheard and recorded the comments made in the playground by some of the staff at the school about some of the children:

Mary Jane? Well, what can you expect – with her being the youngest of nine?

Bilaal – such a lovely child and from such a lovely home.

What was she thinking? Having twins and bringing them up alone. No wonder they are such a handful.

Zena is doing surprisingly well at school.

Innocuous or not? I am sure you can see how in each of these comments there is a tendency to typecast or stereotype the child according to where she lives, what the family is like and so on. Mary Jane is certainly a child from a large family, but is it fair or just to assume certain things on that basis? And why is Zena's success at school surprising just because she lives in a non-traditional family structure?

We know that poverty negatively affects the lives of many children, as does poor health, family trauma and abuse. But to make judgements about a child on the basis of coming from a large or small family, a single parent or nuclear or extended family, a large house or a small flat is unacceptable and implies an inability to treat each child as someone with networks of connections and relationships. We all bring our feelings, relationships and experiences with us into the school or setting. According to Malaguzzi, no one ever comes to anything in an isolated way; we come with 'the pieces of the world attached' to us. This applies not only to children, but also to all the adults who work with them.

Preparing for a day where relationships are key

Paola Strozzi has written an illustrated diary of an ordinary day in the life of the *Scuola Diana* (recently declared by *Newsweek* to be the best nursery school in the world). This diary shows just how the school sets out to create a learning environment where relationships are key (http://emh.kaiapit.net/dailylifeatschool.pdf). It covers the hours from 7.30 am, when the school opens, until 9 am, when all the children have arrived and, together with the teachers, decide what they will be doing that day.

In her introduction to the document, Strozzi tells us that their aim is to create what she calls an 'amiable school'. I love the notion of an amiable school, and ask myself how many young people I know could describe their own schools as being or having been amiable. Malaguzzi said that a school should be a place where the search for the meaning of life and of the future takes place. According to him, such a school would be 'hard-working, inventive, livable, documentable and communicable, a place of investigation, learning, recognition and reflection where the the children, teachers and families are happy' (cited in Strozzi 2001: 58). There is an enormous amount to consider in that description alone.

Walk around the setting where you work or the school your child attends, and and ask yourself if you can see examples of hard work, invention, thinking and learning. Do the children, the teachers and the families seem happy, welcomed and recognised? Are the small and big steps taken by the children each day recorded for the families? And most of all, does it seem to you to be 'liveable'?

The book starts with a series of photographs relating to the *child's arrival at the setting*:

- The first photograph is entitled 'A school that awaits' and shows the sun-filled empty school awaiting the arrival of the children and the teachers. There are plants, children's work on display and everyday and longer term information available to parents. The aim is to create a physical environment that suggests to children and their families stories to be continued or created.

- The second photograph is labelled 'Narrations' and shows one of the document panels that cover the walls 'as if they were a second skin'. Each invites you, the viewer, into the experiences and the stories of the children.
- Next is a photograph labelled 'Saying goodbye' and the accompanying caption tells us that the moment where parents or carers say goodbye to the children is a delicate one, full of meanings and emotions, that will have an impact on the children's sense of well-being as well as that of their parents.

The next set of photographs relates to *preparations for the coming day*:

- First here are photographs showing the teachers greeting one another and exchanging materials and resources in preparation for the day. The relationships between the teachers is important to their own sense of personal and professional well-being, which, in themselves, contributes to the well-being of the children.
- Then there is a detailed exploration of the arrival of some of the 5-year-old children; this is included specially to highlight the importance of the moment where each child is welcomed. The caption reads 'The school is not a place for anonymous users, but for people who live a portion of their lives together'. Marco is one of the children who has been absent for some days and his return is celebrated by a group of his friends who take him into a small room off the classroom because they have a secret to tell him. The photographer respects the children's right to privacy and does not photograph the encounter.

This is followed by a series of photographs illustrating how the building itself *caters for the diverse needs of its users throughout the day*:

- There is a communal central space which mimics the town square or piazza common to towns and cities in Emilia Romagna. This is where children can wait for a friend or gather together to share their ideas, to form groups or move around and change alliances at will.
- There is also explicit recognition that children may need a place where they can be alone if they choose. Smaller spaces allow for this and are often used by both children and adults.
- To illustrate the idea of co-responsibility there are two teachers in each class rather than one. This means that one or other can meet with other adults in the school at any time during the day in order to exchange ideas, seek help or share experiences.

The next section of the booklet shows how the children routinely take items back and forth between home and school, a practice that is regarded as being an essential feature of illustrating how *school and home are in continuity with each other*. For example:

- Each child has a backpack and a place where they can store their belongings.
- There are other personal spaces like message boxes, portfolios for drawings, a storage bin for mail received and more.

The final theme explored is the importance of children being able to *move around, meet and mingle, seek out and play with others*:

- Children are free to roam around the school so, we see, older children can visit younger ones; babies and toddlers are seen crawling up to join a group listening to a story or playing with water, for example.
- Teachers are shown inviting children help set up the tables for lunch time or prepare resources for the coming day.

You might want to read this section again to see if you can see how the booklet/report offers ways in which the setting prepares for a pedagogy of relationship. Your own setting might do it very differently and you might have additional suggestions.

For me the essential things are these:

- The arrival each day of the child plus parent or carer is recognised as being important, so care is taken that what they see when they arrive is attractive and welcoming, and allows them to read small narratives about what the child has been doing.
- Keeping parents informed about all the things the child has been doing is a routine part of the life of the setting.
- The moment of parting is important and should be neither rushed nor stressful. This is sometimes difficult, but it is essential to manage. You might want to consider what you have in place in your setting to help with this.
- Time is found in the planning part of the day for the adults working in the setting to meet and greet one another. Their well-being and sense of belonging to the community of the setting is as important as all other aspects of relationships.
- Individual children are greeted by the adults and the other children; any child who has had something unusual happen has this recognised explicitly. Perhaps a child was ill, went away for the weekend, celebrated a birthday, welcomed a baby sibling or had grandparents visit. The network of relationships impacts on all aspects of the child's life.
- The organisation of space is seen as important in maintaining interaction between children of different age groups in different parts of the setting,

in both large communal and small intimate spaces. There are places where children can keep their personal belongings and places where they can share these if they choose to. Lived life is respected and celebrated.

- Responsibility and expertise are shared so that teachers can leave their own groups to visit others, seek or offer advice or support, contribute to activities throughout the setting, and enjoy the company of their colleagues as well as the children.
- The links between home and setting are so important that space and time are found for them with children bringing in things from home and taking home things from the setting.

Creating a pedagogy of relationships

Those wishing to work with children in a way that considers a pedagogy of relationships need to think about the following:

How to consider each child' s reality

Malaguzzi saw each child as being essentially competent; this competence includes the abilities to communicate and form relationships. These are essential features of being human. Let us look at the realities of the lives of two of the children mentioned earlier in this chapter:

> Zeynep, you will remember, is integrated into a large Turkish community. She has learned how to communicate with her extended family, who speak mainly Turkish. At school the language of learning is English. In her everyday life above the dry cleaning shop she is expected, as a girl, to help her mum in the kitchen. Her mum is a wonderful cook and is inducting the little girl in the secrets of Turkish cuisine. She sees her father reading the Turkish newspapers and listens when he and her grandfather talk about events happening throughout the Arab world. Like families scattered throughout the world, events 'back home' continue to matter enormously for this little family. They are Muslim but rarely go to the mosque. They love Turkish music. The realities of Zeynep's world are multi-layered and complex. She has relationships with both adults and children, with Turkish speakers and English speakers, with the expectations of home (gender-linked, as in helping with the cooking, and more widely to know about events in the world beyond her home) and expectations of learning (to become able to read and write, to be polite, to help in the classroom).

> Zena lives with her two mums, one of whom is training to be a social worker and the other works as a dinner lady at the same school she attends. Her realities are very different from those of Zeynep, although

they do overlap in the playground or on the streets or in the classroom. Zena speaks only one language and her family is small in size and non-traditional in structure. She does not go home after school but to the the after-school club, where she plays games with the other children and is forming relationships with them and with the adults working there. She has to face the challenges of living in a non-traditional family with no father figure to relate to. Her realities include the expectations of her mothers (who want her to become a strong, educated and independent woman when she grows up) and of the classroom (where she, like Zeynep, is expected to become able to read and write, be polite and help in the classroom). Many differences, but some overlap.

Recently the two girls, finding that their first names both began with the letter 'Z', used that as the starting point of what looks as though it could develop into a real friendship.

Those working with young children and thinking about developing a pedagogy of relationships need to know as much as possible about the lived lives of the children so that they understand the complex networks of relationships, communication skills and cultural contexts. They need to know, but not to make judgements.

How to consider each adult's reality

The adults working in any setting are also unique individuals, each with a history and relationships with others, some intense and deeply personal, others less so. For Malaguzzi, their well-being, sense of purpose, understanding of pedagogy and experience are priceless and essential to what happens within the scuole dell'infanzia and nidi. He insisted that all the adults in each centre were called teachers because he understood that in any relationship or exchange teaching and learning are taking place. He also worked over the years to ensure that in each setting there were regular weekly sessions of learning for the adults, usually led by a pedagogista and agreed by the people involved – a pedagogista, you will remember, is the person who coordinates the work of three or four centres. There is no set curriculum as there is in the UK. Children are not expected to meet any targets or goals set by outside agencies. This means that the teachers use what they learn during their in-service training, together with the attentive and analytical observation of what the children are doing, saying and paying attention to, as the basis for setting up and resourcing the activities and planning outside visits. Here are some examples to illustrate this kind of planning and teaching:

Four-year-old Luigi says to one of the adults that the birds outside the window looked bored. When the teacher responds by asking why he thinks they are bored he says that they don't have anything to do. The teacher listens carefully, takes notes and begins to think about where to take this. Luigi has expressed a concern about something he has noticed. The adult interprets this as the child empathising with the birds and internally both raising and answering questions about why this might be so. She decides to take this further, thinking that there is potential in this for much learning – and not only for Luigi.

In an English nursery class the teacher might bring in books with pictures of birds or stories about birds. She might set up a bird table. The children might be asked to draw birds. In Reggio what happened was that the Luigi was invited to tell some of his friends about what he was thinking. The other children were interested and a lively discussion took place with the teacher sitting by, taking notes, sometimes contributing, always ready to respond to what was said. The children decided that what the birds needed were things to play on – the sort of things they found in the parks, gardens and squares of Reggio. They decided they would plan and build playground equipment for birds.

They visited a local playground, taking their drawing materials with them so that they could draw the equipment there. On their return they went out into the garden to choose a possible site for their bird playground. They began to design and draw the things they would make – swings, slides, a roundabout, a climbing frame, a bench to perch on. They then discussed and asked the teacher to make a list of what materials they might need. The list included wood, glue, string, wire, empty cartons, paper clips and more. In the days that followed the children, using their drawings as plans, set about making the playground equipment. There was much discussion about how the things they were making could be made to move, whether they would be strong enough to hold the birds, how many birds could use each piece, how they would be made to stand firmly on the ground. A great deal of problem solving, measurement, estimation, exploration of balance and weight, rotation and movement, was involved, as you can see.

When the playground was ready, one child asked if the teacher thought that the birds liked the playground and this led to another part of the project, where the children began to keep watch on the bird playground, taking turns to count (using a simple system of tallying) the number of birds using each piece of equipment to see which was the most popular.

The cycle went like this:

• The child expressed an idea: the teacher listened attentively.
• A dialogue followed.

- The adult suggested the child share his ideas with friends. The adult observed and recorded what happened.
- The adult arranged for the children to visit a children's playground and organised drawing materials to take on the visit.
- The adult set up possible resources for the children to use in their design and planning.
- The adult recorded what the children said they needed for the next stage.
- All worked to find the resources.
- The children worked alone or collaboratively on their items. The teacher was on hand to interact, support and record.
- Another child expressed a related interest and the planning and doing cycle started again.

The role of the teacher here is that of being attentive to what children say and do, and being willing to use this as the starting point for some work. During the whole process the teacher is involved as a resource: she can write for the children or help them when they encounter something they cannot yet do alone. She can interpret their questions that are not always expressed directly. She can offer words they do not yet have to describe things they want to discuss – rotation, perhaps, or balance. Most importantly she takes notes and photographs so that she has a record of the process for her own interest, to share with her colleagues and with parents and others. It is a thoroughly professional pedagogical role, respecting the children as competent little enquirers with the teacher juggling roles as an observer, follower, initiator, provider, interpreter and recorder of the narratives being made.

Dealing with the unpredictable

Children often come up with unexpected responses and do unpredictable things. Looking at a wordless picture book with Maria, it was baffling when she interrupted her intense concentration on making a narrative from the pictures to say, 'I've got new shoes'. Finding an explanation was challenging. Interpreting comments like this really depends to a large extent on what you, the teacher, know about the child's life, relationships and passions.

When I visited the Reggio schools all those years ago I was told the story of what happened during one of the home-school-home exchanges:

> All children are invited to collect things related to what they do over the long summer break and bring these in when term resumes. The objects provide points for discussion. One little girl brought back a train ticket. When asked what it meant to her, she told the teacher that it made her think of 'arms and legs'. It took a great deal of interest and patience and knowledge of the lived life of the little girl for the adult to work out the explanation. She had visited her grandmother, who lived in a seaside

resort situated high on a hillside. Every day, to get to the beach, they had to walk down a steep street and all she could see were arms and legs.

A pedagogy of relationships implies not only knowing as much as possible about the realities of the lives of the children but knowing who to talk to to help decode and explain the unpredictable or seemingly inexplicable. Do you remember Maria responding to a wordless picture book about a barefoot girl on a beach by saying, 'I've got new shoes'? The teacher, trying to work out why the shoes were so significant, later remembered the child's grandmother telling her that the little girl had been given a new pair of shoes on the day her baby sister was brought home from the hospital.

The unpredictable operates in other ways too. A school or setting, full of people, each an individual tied to others, cannot function like a well-regulated factory – whatever planners and assessors might think. Those working in settings have to be open to what happens and willing to change their plans in response. Malaguzzi says that we need to be 'comfortable with the restless nature of life' (*Exchange* 3:94).

Think about this and you will recognise that this very willingness to be flexible and responsive, rather than in control and rigid, makes the job of teaching more difficult and complex but also potentially far more rewarding. This story comes from a little book called *We write shapes that look like a book* published by Reggio Children, and tells of the relationships children from the nido form with a big old cherry tree near to it:

> The teachers take the children out into the green space and then watch and listen. They notice that the children explore the tree using their senses and interact with it through these explorations and the questions that arise in their heads. The children notice how trails of ants are always present and wonder where they are going. They comment on how the ants follow one another and they explore the tracks the ants make using their fingers. Some children make links with their own experience.
>
> Marco says 'One time I saw a cherry tree at my grandpa's … on the ladder he cut the branches and then he made a pile.'
>
> Rebecca said 'They have cherries attached to them. I go with my grandma to buy them.'
>
> Emanuele said 'My grandpa picks them and puts them in the basket … and I eat them.'
>
> (Cavallini *et al.* 2008: 25)

And Aurora, pressing a little lump of bark, made her own narrative to explain what she found. 'It's a doorbell, it rings where the ants live, there's a hill for the ants. They're here, they're here, they opened the door and here's the den for the ants, scratch to see if there's a little lizard too'.

(Ibid.: 21)

The teachers might well have planned for the children to draw the cherry tree or to dance around it or to pick and eat the cherries. These are all legitimate things to do, but what happened was that they first handed control to the children, watched what they did, listened to what they said and recorded what they saw and heard. They were actively documenting what we might call 'learning on the hoof'. Ask yourselves which is more rewarding – looking, listening, recording and responding, or watching twenty children draw a tree whether they want to or not.

To hand control to the children – especially to these very young ones – requires having a particular view of children, to see them as competent, enquiring, communicating, and able to make and share meanings. They are full partners in any exchange and need to have their feelings, ideas and thoughts respected.

Observation and respect

Rinaldi (2006) talks of how, through observation, adults in the scuole dell'infanzia and nidi have been able to see how important it is to consider things as contributing rather than being opposed to one another. In this way they consider reason and emotion, learning and pleasure, fatigue and joy, oneself and others. This allows for those who spend much of their time together in a setting not only effectively living together for some of the time, but jointly and reciprocally supporting one another. In this environment adults are learning from one another and from the children, just as children are learning from one another and from the adults. Often they become partners in shared and joint enterprises. Here they engage in *respectful reciprocity*.

Bruner said, 'In Reggio one is given to meeting a rare form of courtesy, a precious form of reciprocal respect' (2004: 27). As so often with Bruner, he says so much with a few well-chosen words. Reciprocal respect describes precisely the relationships between all those involved: the children are listened to as though what they say matters, interests the listeners and must be responded to. They learn through this to listen not only to the adults but to other children. Rinaldi sometimes talks of the *pedagogy of listening*, which requires a willingness to listen and pay attention to the ideas, thoughts, feelings and opinions of others – however different they may be from your own.

You may remember that Piaget believed that young children were not able to see the world from any perspective other than their own. In his famous three mountain experiment, young children were asked to choose, from a series of illustrations or photographs, the view that a doll placed somewhere close to the model of three mountains could see. Young children generally failed to do this, choosing instead the image that showed what they could see. Did this mean that they could not put themselves in someone else's shoes and decentre, or did it mean that the question asked made little sense to them? *Hughes* later experimented using a teddy bear hiding from a policeman. He asked the children to identify a picture of what the teddy bear could see. Where the task made some sense to the children and they could draw on their own everyday experience, even young children were perfectly able to decentre. *Judy Dunn*, looking at the social and emotional development of young children, showed how they were perfectly able to intuit the feelings of others and to show empathy – which requires being able to see the world through the eyes of another.

In order to empathise with others and pay attention to their ideas, thoughts and opinions, young children must be able to decentre. To illustrate this, here is a wonderful example drawn from the work of *Vivian Gussin Paley*. She valued the importance of story making, narrative and listening and in her American kindergarten set up a theatre in the classroom. Here is an incident she recorded, which, for me, is reciprocal respect in action.

A group of children, all aged 5, are trying to resolve the difficulty of how to measure two rugs they want to use in their re-enactment of 'Jack and the Beanstalk'. Observe the enormous amount of mathematical thinking going on here. Wally and Eddie disagree about whether the two rugs are the same size or not. It goes like this:

WALLY   The big rug is the giant's castle. The small one is Jack's house.

EDDIE   Both rugs are the same.

WALLY   They can't be the same. Watch me. I'll walk round the rug. Now watch walk, walk, walk, walk, walk, walk, walk, walk, walk – count all these walks. Now count the other rug. Walk, walk, walk, walk, walk. See? That one has more walks.

EDDIE   No fair. You cheated. You walked faster.

WALLY   I don't have to walk. I can just look.

EDDIE   I can look too. But you have to measure it. You need a ruler. About six hundred inches or feet.

WALLY   We have a ruler.

EDDIE   Not that one. Not the short kind. You have to use the long kind that gets curled up in a box.

WALLY   Use people. People's bodies. Lying down in a row.

EDDIE   That's a great idea. I never even thought of that.

(Paley 1981: 13–14)

I just love this extract. How serious the boys are and how carefully they listen to one another. It is a real and equal dialogue. They respect one another's ideas and build on them, and when Wally comes up with the brainwave Eddie is so gracious in his recognition of its brilliance. What Paley does is to pay attention, show respect for and support the children in their imagined worlds, sometimes offering them anchor points to what we might regard as reality (cited in Smidt 2012: 132–3).

Looking back, looking ahead

In this chapter we have examined the idea of a pedagogy of relationships so important to Malaguzzi. It starts with having a view of children and of childhood. For Malaguzzi, the child is always an individual child, situated in the real world, with connections to people within and beyond the home, the neighbourhood, the preschool or infant-toddler group, and the wider world. This is a confident and competent child, wanting to know and understand about the world and the people and objects in it. When that child enters the nido or the scuola dell'infanzia she becomes a full and equal member of this new community and starts to establish relationships with adults and children there. The adults, too, are individuals with histories, living real lives in a world full of relationships. A pedagogy built on relationships is one that takes full account of all those involved in the setting and explicitly recognises the roles they play in the lives and learning of the children. In the next chapter we examine a pedagogy of listening.

Chapter 4

The importance of listening and documentation

> 'Listen children', runs the Yiddish folk song, 'listen with your nose and eyes' and listen we did for in the very next line a cow flew over the old gossip granny's roof.
>
> (Harold Rosen 1964: 6)

We live in a world full of noise and yet we pay very little attention to listening and to its vital role in education. In Reggio Emilia, awareness of the significance of listening went beyond Malaguzzi's earlier musings on the subject to become the stuff of recent books, dissertations and debates. In this chapter we turn our attention to listening and examine what is meant by it, consider children as listeners and teachers as listeners and establish links between listening and assessment and research. You will find links with what has already been said and with what follows. So pay attention and listen with your eyes.

Defining and understanding listening

When I asked some students the question 'What do you think I mean by listening?' they looked at me in puzzlement. The answer seemed so obvious to them, so everyday and ordinary as not to seem worth bothering with:

'It's what you do with your ears,' said one.

'It's what you do with music,' said another.

'You listen to stories, to the radio, to a sound track, to your mother complaining about the mess in your room, to your father boasting about your achievements, to your granny telling you you are the most beautiful person in the world, to the teacher telling you to be quiet, to the wonderful sound of your baby babbling in her cot in the morning, to your lover whispering sweet nothings in your ear.'

So a lot about what you listen to, but little analysis of why listening matters or what it contributes to learning. Let us attempt to go more deeply into the subject and think more carefully about what it is we do when we listen. We will start with a social constructivist view, each illustrated by a small illustration.

Listening is clearly part of our communicative contexts

We listen to other people because we want to know more about them, what they think, what they feel, what they already know. We listen to them to be able to engage in some dialogue with them, so we can share our thoughts, ideas and feelings. We listen to them and they listen to us.

> Rosanna phones her mother and asks, 'How are you feeling today? Are you stronger than you were yesterday? Did your friend visit you? I hope you kept warm, it was so cold'.

We also listen to the narratives that people create and learn from these about what things interest them, what they value, what they believe. Their narratives can be about the past, which may be shared by us or may be very different. Their narratives may be about real life today, similar to or very different from our own.

Listening offers us possible worlds to explore and understanding

> Claudio tells his teacher, 'My mum was very cross and she shouted at me and made me cry. I put my arm on her face and she started to cry too, so we were both crying'.

So listening is something that allows us to recognise that we are part of a social and communicative world. This is as true for the youngest child entering the nido as for a grandmother listening to the gentle sounds being made by her newest grandchild.

Listening is a sensitivity to the patterns that connect us to others

> When I come home in the evenings after work I hear my baby snoring gently in his cot, my wife snoring loudly in our bed and my mother-in-law's snores making the window panes rattle and then I feel safe and normal.

So listening can also be thought of as giving us the capacity to share things with others, moving us out of the isolation of our own thoughts, values and ideas to building shared systems with others.

Listening allows us to create culture with others

We went to hear a lecture about the importance of reading to your children frequently and it was wonderful because everybody there seemed to share the same opinion. It made us feel stronger.

Listening involves many skills

Listening involves an awareness of taking turns, listening to sound and to no-sound, to the silences and the pauses, the hesitations and the gaps, the pulse and rhythms of human communication. There is a pattern here, just as there is a pattern in music or art or poetry.

When my grandfather used to tell us stories we knew that there were moments when the silence meant something scary was going to happen and a different silence that meant something good was going to happen. I don't know how he did it but he made the stories sort of pulse with vitality.

Listening can be to our language, other languages and no language

We listen sometimes to the voices of people who speak a verbal language different from ours and try, as we do so, to find something to allow in, so we can start to comprehend. It may be a gesture, an expression or a tone of voice. So we listen not only to the verbal language but also to other languages that are available in the exchange.

My parents used to speak Yiddish to one another when we were children when they were saying things they didn't want us to understand. Afterwards we would chat together and come to some agreement about what we thought we had heard. We learned quite a lot of words and phrases just doing that. Sometimes it was the lifting of an eyebrow or the emphatic 'Oy vay!' that gave us clues.

Listening allows us to know what others think and feel

We listen to people because we want to know what they think or feel. We are inherently curious and we want to know what questions they ask, what answers they come up with, what further questions this gives rise to and so on.

A child saying, 'It's raining because God is crying' (Rinaldi in Edwards *et al.* 2011: 239) enables the listener to consider what it is the child thinks is happening. The listener can guess at what question has been raised and answered by the child.

Active listening requires time for thought and reflection

In response to the child saying that the rain is God's tears, the listener might have to think carefully about how to respond. I could say, 'I wonder what is making God feel so sad?', 'Perhaps the rain is coming out of the big black cloud?' or 'I love that idea'. How I respond will depend on my own ideas, thoughts and beliefs.

Listening is tied to the emotions, triggered by and triggering them

When my granddaughter was a very little girl and I returned home after being away, she flung her arms around me and hugged me, saying, 'You comed back!' I was happy and moved and sad all at once, and all for different reasons.

Learning and listening

Rinaldi tells us that listening is the premise for any kind of learning relationship. If I asked you if you listen to the children you work with you would certainly say you do – and you would not be lying. But the important question is do you listen attentively, with a real concern to find out what it is that the child wants you to hear? The essence of listening in learning is that it is reciprocal, often initiated by the child because the child has a question, an interest, a theory or a passion and she is turning to you to invite you to share that. Parents are often better at doing this than teachers, partly because they have such a strong relationship with the child and are almost inevitably interested in what the child is saying. When my daughter Sam was a very little girl she said, 'We are oppositting each other, aren't we?' and I was stunned at her inventiveness and replied 'What a wonderful word. Yes. We are sitting opposite each other and you have invented a new word – oppositting. It's wonderful. It says everything in one word. You are clever'. Easy for me because there were no other children requiring my attention at that moment, no learning goals or targets to tick, just the delight of the interaction.

One of the most important things we can learn from Malaguzzi's ideas and those of his successors, like Rinaldi, is the importance in education of this kind of listening. They call it *active listening*. Embedded in the concept of active listening is the idea of it being between equal partners and thus reciprocal. The child has an idea, question or theory and she tells it to you. You listen and in this way she allows you to glimpse what is taking place in her mind. She implicitly invites you to respond in some way. Your responses allow her to confirm or change her idea. It is a wonderful communicative verbal dance.

A group of 4 year olds in Honolulu were outside playing when a gust of wind blew across the yard. 'That's the windy wind', one child said. The teacher asked, 'The windy wind. Are there different kinds of wind?" Soon a gentle breeze wafted across their faces and another child said, 'There, that was a gentle wind'.

(Foreman and Fife in Edwards *et al.* 2011: 260)

Some children aged 3 noticed the shadow of a bird on the floor of the school. At the suggestion of the teacher they drew round it with chalk. Later in the day the bird could still be seen but the shadow was no longer in the same place. The children were intrigued. Then they came up with two possible hypotheses: either the teacher had got it wrong or the bird wanted to move away. They could do nothing about the teacher getting it wrong but perhaps they could find ways of getting the bird to stay with them. They set about testing their hypothesis. Some children tried to build a cage on the floor using tape. Other children tried to tempt the bird to stay by offering it bread crumbs. When nothing worked they went to the class of 4 year olds to seek their advice, but nothing was resolved. A day later, back in their classroom, they noticed that the shadow of the little bird was following the same pathway as it had done on the previous day. They went back to wise Alan, aged just 4. And here is his astounding explanation: 'The sun points his reflection onto the bird because the shadow of the bird knows this road, just as we know the road to go to our house. Early in the morning the shadow is still sleeping. Then the shadow goes into the sun, and the sun points his ray, so that we can see the shadow of the bird. The next day when the sun comes up, the ray understands that is has to go along the same road that it went before.'

(Gandini in Edwards *et al.* 2011: 305–6)

In the first example a question asked by a teacher about something a child had said (evidence that the teacher was really listening) led the children to explore and explain their ideas more clearly. The fact that the child had described the wind as the 'windy' wind was evidence that that child had a theory that there were different kinds of wind in that place. In the second case it was the listening of a child, only very little older than the questioning children, who came up with a wonderful, if scientifically impossible, hypothesis.

Active listening is one of the most important ways in which children are helped to think and question, develop their own hypotheses or theories, express these in some way to the teachers who then respond in a way that helps the child's thinking and learning move on. It is important to remember and keep reminding yourself that questions need not be explicit; they need not be verbal. What children say, do or represent gives you clues into what they are seeking answers to. So you, as teacher, have to listen to their words and their silences, their facial expressions and gestures, their movements and the marks or things they make. Your primary task is to try and work out what the child's question or theory is. See if you can do it in each of these vignettes:

> Samu and Giorgio are playing with the blocks when they see a bug. Samu says, 'It's not moving. Look it's not moving any part of its body'.

> Giorgio says, 'I don't like it. It could sting me even with my pants still on'.

> Oliver tries to sweep up the bug using the small brush and shovel from the sand tray. He taps the bug and listens to the sound the tapping makes.

> Angie starts to draw the bug, using dark coloured crayons and mixing the colours carefully as she works.

> Samu wonders if the unmoving bug is dead. This is often the great unasked question because death continues to be a fascinating and still often taboo area.

> Giorgio asks if it could sting him through his trousers. Perhaps he has been stung in the past and so is nervous.

> Oliver realises that the others are not keen to have the bug close to them so he finds a way to move it and then taps on its shell and listens to the sound it makes. Perhaps he is asking what the shell is made of, if it is hard or not and what purpose it serves. His actions show his ability to empathise with the anxieties or dislikes of others.

> Angie tries to represent the bug, paying attention to the colours of its shell. Perhaps she is asking how to make a particular mixed colour or why the bug has a shell of that colour. Malaguzzi was clear that what children learn is often not what teachers set out to teach them. What they learn arises from being able to follow their own interests and the responses teachers make in recognition of this.

The emphasis is on the child as initiator and the interaction is only successful for the child's learning when the teacher can respond appropriately, sometimes verbally or with physical help, offering resources or in other ways. How teachers respond is totally dependent on their active listening.

The child as social being

We don't set out to teach children to be social any more than we teach them to be speakers of their own language. Living in a social world with other people, they are intensely interested in other people and in the things that other people say, do and make. Their interest is what allows them to be drawn into their culture and the ways in which people have found of communicating. Vygotsky called these 'cultural tools': books, paintings, pens, paintbrushes, musical instruments, music itself and much more. Even very young children get drawn into expressing their thoughts and feelings and ideas in any and every way. This takes time and involves pleasure and excitement but also patience and sometimes struggle. Rinaldi thinks that what a school should primarily be about is a context for what she calls *multiple listening*. The children listen to one another, they listen to the teachers and the teachers listen to one another and to the children. One child might speak to another child or to a group of children. It is a complicated chain of listening. Through this it becomes possible for the child to be in charge of her own learning in the sense of being able to follow her interests, ask or answer her questions, suggest her theories, not alone, but as part of a community of listeners and responders.

The learning process looks something like this. The child, interested in or curious about something, develops an internal mental image of it. Perhaps she has seen an ant carrying a large crumb across the floor. The child retains a mental picture of this and once she develops the use of spoken language, perhaps a verbal image of it. To share this with others she can explain it, draw it, paint, it, make it out of clay, move like it, act it out and in this way shift from one language to another. The child in isolation might learn from using many languages in this way, but the social child with opportunities of sharing this with others – peers and adults – has the possibility of listening and being listened to: hearing the thoughts of others; making comparisons; respecting differences; and accepting suggestions. So the social child learning with others uses different languages herself and shifts between languages in her *reciprocal exchanges* with others. In this way, concepts and *conceptual maps* are formed and consolidated.

Rinaldi suggests that, in situations like this, the child learns how to learn and the group becomes aware of its own role as a teaching place. You may be familiar with Bruner's idea of *scaffolding*, where, he believes, a more expert person is able to make the novice in any situation take small supported steps towards more independent thinking. Although this is a plausible, often cited and certainly very real feature of learning, it is situated in the classic idea of schooling being about dyads or pairs – child and adult or more expert child. In Reggio, the concept is more social and becomes one of *reciprocal expectations*. Thus the ideas and suggestions, or even criticisms, of others in the group can contribute to learning.

If you think about this you will see that is has really significant implications for teachers. What they have to do is become careful, analytical and knowledgeable documenters. In order to understand and interpret each interaction they are documenting they need to be able to draw on what they know about how children learn and develop. You will remember that all teachers have continuous ongoing staff development as part of their conditions of employment – learning about child development and about how to interpret what is seen and heard in light of this is a large part of their programmes.

Rinaldi describes documenting as *visible listening*. Teachers keep track of everything seen and heard through using notes, photographs, videos and slides and, in this way, are able to make visible to everyone the relationships that they see as the building blocks of knowledge.

Internal listening

Hoyuelas, who studied Malaguzzi's thoughts and words very carefully, explains the importance for the child of working with small groups. He cites what Malaguzzi said about this in *La Storia, Le Idee, La Cultura* (2006: 107–8). The child, familiar with interactions with adults and perhaps with one or two other children, experiences these relationships in the prescribed and possibly narrow context of the everyday, the home and the family. When the child begins to work with unknown or less well-known children, in small groups in the preschool the child begins to consider her relationship and position in these groups. When the child finds that her ideas are different from those of others she begins to realise, possibly for the first time, that she actually does have her own ideas. Conversely she discovers that others, too, have their own ideas. I love the answer children gave to a question put to them by Malaguzzi, who asked, 'When is someone a friend?' The answer given was 'When you know his name'. Malaguzzi's analysis was that this meant more than merely attaching a label to a face but knowing the person's body, gestures, voice, skin, eyes and attitudes.

I have talked about listening and about visible listening. We now turn our attention to *internal listening*. It will make sense to you that, as a child shares an idea or thought with another, she also becomes more aware of that idea herself. It is the old idea that you are only secure in your own ideas when you have to teach them to someone else. So each time the child moves from using one language to another, one group to another, one experience to another, she reflects on each and may change, modify or abandon her original thesis. Here are some examples, all drawn from Vecchi's book (2010), to make this clear:

> A little girl called Sewaa is being the model for children who want to draw or model her in clay. The session starts with the children talking

about what Sewaa looks like. She responds to what they say and joins in with their comments, some of which are about skin colour. Filippos suggests that Theo likes Sewaa because they have the same skin. Camilla replies that that can't be true because she likes Evans and he has brown skin. Sewaa puts them all straight by saying 'I like Theo because he's my friend and I like Ismail who was nearly my friend. ... So skin colour has nothing to do with it!' It is possible that this comment might make one or more children review their hypotheses and either confirm or change them.

At times children get up to look at and critique one another's work. Laura tells Martina that her drawing is wrong because she is drawing a frontal view instead of the profile view she can see from where she is sitting. The teacher, listening closely, comes over to admire Martina's drawing and to ask gently where Martina would have to be sitting for Sewaa to be full-face.

(Vecchi 2010: 50–52)

A group of 5 and 6 year olds explore the space in the building that becomes the Loris Malaguzzi Centre. They spend most of their time in two empty rooms with two rows of parallel columns. One child comments 'These columns are beautiful but they are too similar. Each column is a column.' They decide to design garments for each column to make each one distinct and individual. As they work they comment on what they are doing: When shapes are being cut out there is a problem fitting them together. Alessandro says 'We need to cut less'. Another child, Paolo, noticing that his is still not a perfect fit says 'I didn't cut right down to the end, otherwise this piece in the middle would have come away and wouldn't be nice there and it wouldn't be as nice'.

As they work the children observe and discuss, evaluate their own work and that of others. They combine and share, agree and copy. All the time they are firming up their own ideas and assessing themselves in terms of what they are trying to do. So this internal listening is tied to self-awareness and self-evaluation.

Recently, as children have become more familiar with aspects of technology like digital cameras, they are more and more not only assessing and evaluating their own learning, but also documenting it. Vecchi suggests that children are reflective and honest about their own work and teachers should be careful to be respectful of this and not offer empty praise or negative comments. I am reminded of the story of little Nicola, new to the nursery class, taking her finished painting off the easel to show to the teacher, to be told by her more experienced friend Sally: 'Don't bother. She'll just tell you it's beautiful'.

Documentation

Documentation is really at the heart of the whole Reggio Emilia enterprise. It is a more complex and nuanced type of documentation than we are used to. Certainly in many of the nurseries and other settings in the UK, teachers keep notes and records, they sometimes and in some ways share these with the children and even with the parents, but it seems more of an add-on than an essential part of the teaching and learning process.

Listening, looking, taking notes and interpretation are woven together so that one thing is not possible without the others. Once you have looked and listened you need to record what you saw and heard and then you need to think about it. You think about in light of what you know about the individual child or the group of children, and what you know about child development. You analyse your observation using the ideas of those who have gone before and whose thinking you like. We have seen how Malaguzzi was persuaded by the ideas of thinkers like Vygotsky, Bruner, Howard Gardner and others. Malaguzzi's successors like Vecchi and Rinaldi are in turn influenced by Malaguzzi's ideas. The records once made are then available to be shared, which opens up a whole new range of possible interpretations.

In their paper on documentation, *Turner and Wilson* (2009) discuss how it operates with three key people in Reggio Emilia: *Carlina Rinaldi*, Pedagogical Director of the Municipal Infant-Toddler Centres and Preschools for many years, *Tiziana Filippini*, Coordinator of the Documentation and Educational Research Centre of Reggio Emilia, and *Sandra Piccinni*, President of the Infant-Toddler Centres and Preschools of Reggio Emilia. For Filippini, documentation is more than a tool; it is an attitude towards teaching and learning. This relates closely to Malaguzzi's idea that teachers are like archaeologists who come home in the evenings with their finds and examine all the notes and jottings they have made. They do this precisely so that they can position what they have found in a place, time and culture. In doing this, they establish some relationships with what they have found. In a sense, the very process of documentation increases the knowledge of the teacher. The teacher knows more about how the children learn, about their behaviours and her relationships to them. She is, in Rinaldi's words, effectively writing the stories that tell us who the children are, what they are interested in, what questions they are asking and why, how they set about solving problems, expressing feelings, joining in, working alone or in a group. The stories are about the children as co-constructors of culture; actors in society and citizens

If you are ever fortunate enough to visit Reggio Emilia you will see the stories prominently displayed and can also encounter samples of them in the many books written about Reggio itself. The documentation is carefully arranged and organised, using transcriptions of children's conversations and remarks, photographs of ongoing work and activities, and the products that have been produced by the children to represent their thinking and learning. Alongside this you will find teachers' commentaries on the purposes of a project, along with transcriptions of children's verbal language. Photographs and representations of their thinking are provided in accompanying panels or books designed to present the children's learning processes.

The documentation shows several key things to different people:

- Children see that their work is valued;
- Parents have evidence that their children have been engaged in individual and group activities and experiences;
- Teachers are enabled to assess both their teaching and the children's learning;
- Dialogue is fostered with other educators;
- A historical archive is created that traces pleasure in the process of children's and teachers' learning experiences (drawn on Gandini 1993).

The teachers are eager to use various forms of representation of what the children have learned; these include:

- Sketches of children's work as part of their field notes;
- Photographs of classroom experiences;
- Audio-taped transcriptions of conversations with children.

Teacher's observations and transcribed tapes, which may be taken to colleagues for group reflection. As New (1992: 17) tells us:

> as teachers engage in 'collaborative reflection (so that outcomes are often in the form of collective understandings) ... they socially construct new knowledge as they investigate, reflect, and represent children's construction of knowledge.'

Looking back, looking ahead

In this chapter we have started to look at the importance of listening to learning. We have considered children as listeners to one another and to their teachers, and the listening of teachers to one another and to the children. So listening becomes something shared and reciprocal. We have seen how important this is in allowing teachers a window into the interests and concerns of children, as well allowing children to become aware of their own learning. We ended the chapter by looking at the role of documentation, which is a theme we return to again and again in this book. In the next chapter we start to think about the ways in which children express their ideas, through what Malaguzzi famously called their 'hundred languages'.

Chapter 5

The hundred languages of children

The child
is made of one hundred.
The child has
a hundred languages
a hundred hands
a hundred thoughts
a hundred ways of thinking
of playing, of speaking.
A hundred, always a hundred
ways of listening
of marvelling of loving
a hundred joys
for singing and understanding
a hundred worlds
to discover
a hundred worlds
to invent
a hundred worlds
to dream.
The child has
a hundred languages
(and a hundred hundred hundred more)

(Loris Malaguzzi, translated by Leila Gandini)

If you ask people what they know about Reggio Emilia and its preschools they will almost certainly mention the hundred languages of children. This is the name now given to the exhibition originally called *L'Occhio Se Salta Il Muro: Narrativa del possibile* when it was first presented in 1984. The title means 'when the eye jumps over the wall' and the subtitle tells us that it is a narrative of the possible. Making sense of the title is difficult, but, in the book that was published with this first exhibition, Malaguzzi set out sixteen points relating to what the exhibition showed. The first point gives us the answer to the meaning of the title.

Here Malaguzzi says that the title is hopeful, in the sense that the eye leaping over the wall makes us think about how important it is to consider new and ever-changing cultural roles played in an ever-changing world. In the new asili and scuole dell'infanzia children were and still are being asked to question, to research, to collaborate, to make and represent and re-represent using all the means at their disposal. Adults, too, are having to change their roles as they initiate and respond, research and document, learn and teach. The wall of the title is that of incongruity, banality, old and worn-out rules, pre-packaged concepts and rhetorical actions that accompany outdated ways of thinking about children and childhood, learning and development.

The first part of Malaguzzi's poem (cited at the start of this chapter) tells us that the child has numerous ways of experiencing, representing and re-representing her ideas and thoughts. With these hundred languages, thoughts and hands the child plays, speaks, listens, marvels, sings, understands, discovers the real world and invents and dreams other worlds. These are the capabilities that Malaguzzi wants to see unleashed in children in these early years of learning and development.

What is meant by the hundred languages?

The simple answer to this question could be a list of the ways in which children are able to express their ideas, thoughts, feelings, questions and emotions: by drawing, painting, making, singing, dancing, acting and becoming; by using their bodies to touch, smell, taste, listen to, move, stroke, feel or envelop; by using words, paintbrushes, pencils, chalk, paint, clay, mud, stones, mirrors, spades, string and more. And this is what we 'outsiders' are able to experience of the hundred languages – the wonderful graphic and other images the children create, and the intriguing questions they ask as they explore the world. But this is only the visible or tangible – the final product that usually arises out of a complex and often long-term engagement with a question or a problem that the child has been investigating, alone or with others. What interests me most is the journey taken and the reasons for the journey.

If, as Malaguzzi says, the purpose of the journey of education is not to acquire a body of knowledge but rather to question, consider and challenge the boundary between the mundane, banal and often trivial requirements of schooling as we think of it and the possible world of new ideas, the hundred languages could not be put to better use.

Let us look at some examples to clarify this, drawn from the work of Foreman (in Edwards *et al.*, 2011: 348–55).

At *La Villetta School* in Reggio Emilia the teachers often took the children out into the city to explore its urban and green spaces, its streets and squares, homes and shops, parks and garden. The children had been talking about what the effect of rain on their city might be. They had planned to take photographs of familiar and new places and make guesses about how rain would change them. But that year the seasonal rains were very late in arriving so children had a lot of time to think about what materials and tools they would need to ask and answer their questions. They talked about taking photographs which needed cameras and a printer; they thought of things they might collect or measure or record. They compared their questions: How deep would the puddles be? What things might float on them? What things would be reflected in them? What new things might grow?

When the rainstorm first broke the children were very excited and noticed things no one had anticipated. People changed their speed and posture when walking in the rain; the shiny streets and reflections changed the familiar and made it seem quite different; raindrops made varying sounds when falling on the pavement from falling on the cars or on leaves on the trees. The children began to draw and paint, make stories, design waterproof clothing, measure the depth of puddles, collect things that floated and those that sank. They fashioned trees in clay and tried to make them look wet.

Forman and his colleagues documented the project, which became known as the *City in the Rain* project. It began in a manner that has become standard in Reggio Emilia, a type of verbal outpouring of children's ideas. From where does the rain come? How does the rain sound as it hits different surfaces? What in the city is built because of the rain? How is rain harnessed for good uses? Then, as the children waited for the first rain, they drew their ideas on large poster paper. Some drew their theories of the rain's source: 'The devil makes it rain,' said one 5 year old. Another insisted that 'the rain is made by big machines in the sky, and the rain goes into the clouds, and when the clouds are too full the rain falls out.' These drawings were the children's initial theories about the rain cycle and they served as a platform from which to discuss and expand the children's understanding. The project in Reggio Emilia continued for many weeks, including such activities as: making audiotapes of the rain sounds on different surfaces and then making a graphic rendering of these sounds; going into the city filled with questions that had been raised from the classroom discussions and drawings; drawing machines that could make rain; drawing a system of water works that bring the rain water from the sky to the ground to pipes to homes; using a sequence of photographs that show a changing sky and then drawing these changes on paper; drawing a city before and during a rainfall, and drawing many more examples of multi-symbolic learning; (Edwards *et al.*, 2011: 348–55).

Compare that with the way in which an urban English nursery class responded to rain after a dry period. This account comes from a set of observation notes made by a student teacher:

After the rain – it was a real storm – the children were very excited and wanted to go out and see the puddles. The teacher made them all put on their coats and outdoor shoes and took them into the playground. There was one enormous puddle and the children kept trying to jump into it. Two children got shouted at for getting their shoes wet. Another child started to put bits of paper into the puddle, watching to see what happened. The teachers stood talking to one another. I overhead Jacob saying, 'Look, I can see myself in it. Like a mirror, but I look upside down.' No one took a blind bit of notice. The only question raised by any of the adults was 'What sound does puddle start with? And water? And wet?' I thought it a total waste of an opportunity. The children were interested, questioning, noticing, communicating, but the teachers were only thinking about the next lesson, which was phonics. It was that that made me decide that teaching was not for me.

Another project began in the *Anna Frank School* when an outbreak of dinosaur mania hit the children. Noticing the developing obsession with toy dinosaurs, stories about dinosaurs and cartoons about them on television, the teachers decide to suggest that the children work on building dinosaurs. The project start with a lot of discussion about dinosaurs: when they had lived, if there were male and female dinosaurs, what were the differences between male and female, how did they have babies, what did they eat, what killed them and more. No living person has seen a dinosaur. They are like a fictional character. Where boundaries between the accepted and the possible are crossed it is acceptable to ask questions about anything at all.

The first stage involved two small groups – one of boys and one of girls, choosing a dinosaur to make together with the materials to make it. Both groups decided to make Tyrannosaurus Rex and the girls chose to make their model out of Styrofoam and the boys out of wire and metal. After the completion of these models the children continued to talk about two things that interested them: size and dimension.

The adults decided to exploit this interest and asked a small group of children if they could find a way of making a life size dinosaur and hanging it so that its feet touched the ground. The children wanted to know how big a real Tyrannosaurus had been and they were astounded to find illustrations of the creature next to a human being. The teacher read out that an adult Tyrannosaurus Rex was 27 metres high. The children were familiar with metre sticks so they set out to find them in the school. They only found two. It seemed to be the end of the project, but then the atelierista, Roberta, suggested they go into the studio to look for alternative long things to use. They found some plastic rods used to hang paintings from. Each was roughly the same length as the metre sticks. They then decided that the internal space was too small and decided to lay out the dimensions in the sports field in front of the school When they ran out of plastic rods they ran back inside and returned with toilet paper.

This is only part of the story told by Rankin (cited in Edwards *et al.* 2011), but it serves to illustrate the languages the children were using and the role the adult was playing.

> The children arrived with questions in their heads and in a community which promotes the saying '*Io che siamo*', which means 'I am who we are', knew that they could raise these questions within the school community. The culture is that of working together, sharing thoughts and ideas and resources, helping one another, knowing how to get help, and not being scared to have a go. The adults answered the questions or helped the children find ways to answer them. The children here were not engaged in making something pretty or attractive: they were interested primarily in exploring size and dimensions. The adult then set them a challenge – to build something the same size as a dinosaur had been. So here the languages the children used included measuring, estimating, comparing, searching for resources, evaluating what they found, working together. The children did succeed – with much help and encouragement, but always on their own terms, in building a huge creature which actually did fit into the dimensions they had defined.

This describes a very small part of a prolonged project that involved the children in many activities, outings, questions, answers, partial answers, trial and error, success and failure, more questions, asking for help, getting help, working alone and working together. When you read what the teachers in Reggio Emilia say about any of the documented projects you find this impressive delving into issues – some simple, some complex – in depth, over time and using everything to hand.

Creating an inclusive community

Ivana Soncini (cited in Edwards *et al.* 2011) was a member of the Pedagogical Coordinating Team of the Istitutzione Preschools and Infant-Toddler Centres of the Municipality of Reggio Emilia. She held responsibility for inclusion of children with special rights in the municipal scuole dell'infanzia and nidi. It is interesting first to note that the term used is *children with special rights* and not *children with special needs*. This says a great deal about how such children are regarded. As a trained psychologist, she works with all the preschools in Reggio and follows Malaguzzi's insistence that children with special rights be included in what we might call mainstream provision. His focus was on improving pedagogical experience and understanding of all children by doing this.

The way this is done is by welcoming and not ignoring the concept of differences among children, and learning from these children. Malaguzzi believed that teachers would be stimulated to think more carefully about their teaching when they considered the responses of these children as well as their needs. For him, it would give more proof that there is not one way to teach, not one approach that will benefit all children. Homogeneous methods will not work. Children with a special right are identified early in Reggio, usually soon after birth, and they are included in preschool provision as soon as a diagnosis has been made. In fact, these children have absolute precedence over all other children in terms of admissions. In a chapter she wrote in Edwards *et al.* (2011), Soncini describes what the main kinds of disabilities were seen in young Reggio children. These included Downs Syndrome, motor disabilities including paralysis, psychosis, schizophrenia, autism, blindness, deafness, developmental delay owing to chromosomal abnormalities and emotional and psychological difficulties. Today, by contrast, more than half of young Reggio children are diagnosed with autism or autistic spectrum disorder, and most of the remainder have cognitive or intellectual disabilities.

We will look at one child, 5-year-old Matteo who has autism spectrum disorder and has been attending the La Villetta scuola dell'infanzia since he was 3. To begin with, he did not speak and used to throw things. Now he is calmer. Here is an account of an incident and how it was handled by the teachers. It is offered for you to consider in the sense of how a child missing the most common of the hundred languages, verbal language, can be supported in his learning and development:

It is snack time. The supporting teacher sets out three chairs and a stool in front of the benches where most of the children are sitting. Matteo is encouraged to sit close to the teacher, facing the other children. He touches her face. Rosie takes him by the hand, guides him to the kitchen to prepare a plate of fruit. She carries the plate and he follows her. He gets the fork from the plate and moves away from her. The teacher intervenes to stop him while Rosie asks him 'Where are you going?' They return to stand in front of the children and Matteo sits on a chair between the teacher and Rosie.

The teacher then asks Matteo to call out some friends, presenting him with one card at a time, each with a photo of one child on it. Matteo looks at each picture, then at the children in front of him, then calls out the name of the pictured child. One by one the friends come up to spear a piece of fruit from the plate. When Matteo gets distracted Rosie pats his face. Every time he says a name the teacher or one of the children shouts out something in praise. When he says the name of a child who is absent Rosie says, 'Look', and when he looks and does not see the child present, he replies, 'At home', at which point he is again praised by his peers or the teacher. When he comes to his own picture he says, 'Io, io!' (which means, 'It's me!'). Rosie gives him a hug and it is his turn to spear a piece of fruit.

(Soncini in Edwards *et al.* 2011: 198)

When teachers are faced with communicating with children who do not have or use verbal language, they have an absolute responsibility for interpreting the alternative ways in which the child communicates. Teachers doing this discover that every child has her own individual timing and strategies for learning. Here is another child, with a different disability; see how the teachers were able to broaden his palette of languages:

> Enrico was diagnosed with a general psychomotor delay due to an unnamed genetic condition. He was very small for his age but his motor skills were good. He had no oral communication but understood much of what was said to him and he had developed his own system of signing. When his nursery got involved in getting the children to consider what they thought about Reggio itself the teachers worked hard to enable Enrico to contribute. The teachers had taken photographs of the children on an outing in the town and showed these on a screen. They asked Enrico to indicate what he liked about Reggio and told him he could point, draw or use sounds. His response was fascinating as he focused on the sounds in the town. For example he pointed to a saxophone player on a street corner. Offered a choice of languages he was able to communicate.

One of the most moving things Soncini says is that it is the children who often find solutions which they offer to the teachers, in terms what would help children with special rights. As Malaguzzi said, 'Things about children and for children are only learned from the children.' Inclusion is a two-way process with benefits for all. Here is one more case history to illustrate this:

> Umberto at first could not sit up so he spend much of his time lying down. The teachers found he had very low tolerance for being touched on his hands, but not on his face. The teachers encouraged the children in the class to interact and form relationships with him. One day they noticed two little girls listening to soft music, start gently pulling different coloured pieces of gauze over this face and playing bells for him. He showed his pleasure at the interactions with these girls by smiling and clapping his hands and making noises.

(Soncini, in Edwards *et al.*, 2011)

Papatheodorou   (www.tactyc.org.uk/pdfs/Reflection-Papatheodorou.pdf) visited Reggio Emilia and was impressed by much of what she saw, but noted that during her visit there was no mention of disadvantage or additional needs, and wondered if this was because these issues were regarded as having been successfully dealt with or because there was a different attitude to them. I agree with her that one cannot transpose the Reggio model to other cultures, and believe that one of the things that makes Reggio Emilia so interesting is its very focus on the shared, the collective and the collaborative rather than on the individual. Children working together are the norm and this applies to those with differences of all kinds.

Questioning, challenging and transgression

The hundred languages of children are vital in enabling them to become full citizens of their own communities. To be a full citizen of any community it is necessary to be able to understand what you encounter and experience, to evaluate it, to challenge it if it does not meet your requirements or accept your values and to work to change it. You will remember that when the first preschool provision was set up all those years ago the women, fighting for their rights, were also fighting for the rights of their children. What they were determined to see was some sort of education that would not maintain the status quo, but challenge it so that the children coming from poverty could get out of poverty: those coming with few opportunities could be enabled to find more. One of the most important ways of becoming able to critique and challenge is to know that transgression can be a tool.

The definition of transgression is often tinged with a suggestion of sin. I use it in the sense of breaking rules, challenging existing norms and practices and knowing that it is acceptable to do this.

In the *City in the Rain* progettazione the children were implicitly given permission to get their feet and their hands wet. They were not nervous of getting into trouble for doing this. They were invited to suggest their ideas and try out their developing hypotheses. One child threw small things and then larger things into the puddle, interested in noticing if the patterns made change as the object changed. One child collected things that floated and those that did not. Two children worked together using chalk on the paving stones to try and recreate the reflections seen in the puddles. In the dinosaur project the questions raised by the teachers and the children often touched on subjects that in other places might be regarded as 'unsuitable' – questions around gender, birth and death, for example. So when the teachers asked the children where they thought baby dinosaurs came from, they implicitly gave the children permission to talk about their ideas concerning procreation. Similarly, when they talked about whether there were both male and female dinosaurs and invited the children to think about how they would know which was which, they again gave permission for talking about aspects of gender. These large issues are often of interest to children and are just as often taboo subjects at home or in the community.

Children's theories

Both Rinaldi and Vecchi document some of the theories they have witnessed young children developing. Bruner, on visiting one of the scuole dell'infanzia, was astounded to observe many of the teachers sitting and listening to the children talk about their theories. Here are some of the things children have been heard to say. Play the role of the teacher and decide what their theory is, and then think of what you might say, suggest or provide in order to help them develop this theory. They are all drawn from quotations in the books by one of the atelieristi, Vea Vecchi.

> Alice: I wonder where they get all the colours from. Perhaps they collect lots of dead butterflies and make the colours from their wings. No, perhaps they use grasses.
>
> (2010: 29)

> Giorgio: When I made the plant I was thinking about its energy, because it has an energy that makes it grow with its roots, with water and light.
>
> (2002: 70)

> Federica: To make the transformation you have to have two different things: one thing becomes another thing.
>
> (2012:65)

> Giovanni: Look, something that big can hold the ideas of all the kids. Not just one idea but lots of ideas.
>
> (Ibid.: 39)

How did you get on? It is easier to work out what the child's theory is than to know how to work with the child to take it forward and that is primarily because I am asking you to do this without context or history. You know nothing about the children or their experience. Knowing the children and their history you would find this much easier. This demonstrates the importance of context, history and culture once again.

Here are what some student teachers said in response to this:

> Alice is trying to work out where the colours in the world come from. I would guess it relates to using paints and crayons. I would respond by saying something about how many colours we can find in nature (butterflies, flowers and so on) and then get her to try making colours perhaps from petals. I guess it could lead to having lots of fun mixing colours.

> That Giorgio sounds really bright. He understands a lot about what living things need need in order to grow and he makes links with growth

and energy. I would have to take advice on this but thought it could lead to doing work with growing plants and trying things like putting some in a dark place, depriving some of water and so on. I also thought we could do some simple experiments – the children could do them – with batteries and bulbs. I would quite like to ask him to draw energy, just to see what he would do. Perhaps, learning from Reggio (where, I read, they often choose to work with small groups of children), I could get three children to work together to draw energy.

Federica: I love her using the word transformation but I guess that is because she has lots of experience of thinking about how things change. I would love to talk to her about what things she has seen change. Perhaps I could ask her and some friends to use what they find in the classroom to transform themselves. This could become a really big project. Change is such an interesting idea!

I was baffled by Giovanni's comment but then someone told me it was what he said when he went into the theatre. So then it made sense. I love the thought that a space – a theatre, holds ideas, like a library holding books. I would like to get him to draw a space with ideas in it.

And here, just to delight and perhaps confuse you, is a real example of a child's theory about numbers and how they work. I overheard this on a London bus in 2012:

CHILD Mum, I am going to give you two numbers and you have to add them.
MUM   Fine.
CHILD What is four and seven?
MUM   Eleven. [Child, outraged, started screaming.]
CHILD No, no! Don't be silly. I gave you two numbers to add and you told me the answer is only one number. That can't be right.

My analysis is the child thinks that if you add two numbers together the answer must be bigger than two numbers. Eleven is just one number and the child does not yet know that what is being added together is the contents, if you like, of each numeral. So to her mind adding one number (four) to another number (seven) must make the answer more than just another number (eleven). Her theory is that if you add two numerals together the answer must consist of at least three numerals. It is perfectly logical if not mathematically correct, and I have been wondering ever since about what I would have put in place for her to help her build on and transform, abandon or elaborate her theory.

Little researchers

The children, from the youngest ones in the nidi, to the older ones on the verge of leaving the scuole dell'infanzia, are continually looking, listening and raising questions. The questions are only rarely expressed. Mostly it is the children's behaviour that lets us know what it is they are paying attention to and inquiring into.

Here are some examples from the youngest children. See if you can ask the question you think the child is asking:

> Jacopo, in the playground, holds a leaf up to show his friend. He says, 'It's a leaf ... there's a hole'.

> Silvia, playing with clay, makes shapes and says, 'I'm writing'.

> In a discussion the children start to talk about how long a road they want to make should be. The children decide to measure the distance by all standing in a long line and spreading their arms and legs wide, then holding hands.

Here are more complex and well-hidden questions being raised by the children's behaviour rather than words:

> Alessi peers into the puddle, seeing his reflection he walks round and round, looking down all the time. He climbs onto a step and looks down from a greater height. He pulls Giorgio to stand beside him and they both look into the reflection.

> Livia spots a trail of ants going across the path. She watches intently and gasps when one of the ants picks up a very large breadcrumb. Another ant comes over to help carry. She watches for a long time.

> The children are invited to draw one of their classmates in profile. One child draws then moves to a different position and draws again. She then goes over to get some clay and reproduces the image using clay, first from one side and then from another.

A group of student teachers responded as follows:

> Jacopo might be asking what made the hole in the leaf.

> Silvia seems to be asking if her shapes do look like real letters.

The children measuring the road seem to be asking if they can use their bodies to measure very big things.

Alessi seems to be asking if his reflection stays the same or changes.

Livia is interested in the ants and how they can carry such big objects. A how and perhaps a why question.

The children drawing one another in profile seem to be asking if the images changes according to where the observer is standing.

Now see if you can think of ways of using these questions as the start of a longer and more in-depth project.

This time the responses come from experienced teachers:

Arvind said, 'In response to the interest in the leaf with a hole in it, I think I might start a project on silkworms. They are easy to keep and the children can watch as they change. They can see all the stages and draw what they said. We could back it up with books like *The Very Hungry Caterpillar*. The children could make their own silkworms in the form of soft sculptures. We might be able to start a wormery'.

Rochelle added, 'I love the thought of a long term project on letter-like shapes. We could make them with our bodies. We could make them out of different materials – clay, mud, in wet sand, using paints, soft sculpture. We could explore the different kinds of shapes of the letters in other languages and look at curls and dots and straight lines. We would make patterns of repeated letter shapes or make real words or spell out names. We could do them very large in the playground or garden, or tiny. We could back it up with posters of alphabets from different languages and invite people from the local community in to illustrate their letters. We could paint them with delicate paintbrushes. We could invent pictograms. It could go on and on forever!'

Amber added, 'Reflection is a great subject and something children have experience of and an interest in. We could do loads with mirrors and with light. We could do self-portraits. We could give children hand held mirrors to use outdoors and in their drawings. We could use reflective surfaces that are flat or curved to see what happens to the reflections. We could talk about upside down and topsy-turvy and left and right. We could do mirror writing'.

We have strayed from the hundred languages of children to the equal number of languages teachers use in noting, considering and planning from the children's interests. You will find more of this in the next chapter.

Looking back, looking ahead

In this chapter we have been thinking about what Malaguzzi thought and meant about the hundred languages of children. We have seen how he regarded them as seekers of meaning, communicators asking questions as well as trying to answer them, coming up with hypotheses and forming their own theories and, in doing all of this, being willing to take chances, get things wrong and sometimes do the unexpected or the unaccepted. In the next chapter we turn our attention to what the teachers must do to help the children find and use these languages. The implication is that they, too, need a hundred languages.

Chapter 6

The hundred languages of teachers

> To learn and relearn together with the children is our line of work. We proceed in such a way that the children are not shaped by experience but are the ones who give shape to it. There are two ways in which we can look into children's learning process and find clues for supporting it: one is the way children enter into an activity and develop their strategies of thought and action; the other is the way in which the objects involved are transformed. Adults and children go about their learning differently: they use different procedures, honour different principles, make different conjectures and follow different footprints.
>
> (Malaguzzi in Edwards *et al.* 2011: 61)

Like many people across the world, I first became aware of the work of Loris Malaguzzi in 1984, when I bought a small book titled *L'Occhio se Salta il Muro: Narrative of the Possible*. The book was published after an exhibition of the work done by teachers and children in the Reggio preschools called 'The Hundred Languages of Children'. First shown in Sweden, it then toured the world. What interested and astounded people was the quality of the children's creative work. Later Malaguzzi wrote that it is not only children who have the hundred languages, but also their teachers, which is what I will explore in this chapter. We will look at how teachers need to redefine their roles so that they are more than conveyors of knowledge and supporters of children. They are creators and sustainers of relationships; they are researchers; they must learn to follow children's time and interests; they must sometimes think ahead, be the chief protagonist, invent, prompt, design, create, be the audience and the listener, the arbiter and judge, the author and scribe, the listener and recorder.

Do you remember the poem at the beginning of the previous chapter? Here is the second part:

but they steal ninety-nine.
The school and the culture
separate the head from the body.
They tell the child:
to think without hands
to do without head
to listen and not to speak
to understand without joy
to love and to marvel
only at Easter and at Christmas.
They tell the child
to discover the world already there
and of the hundred
they steal ninety-nine.
They tell the child:
that work and play
reality and fantasy
science and imagination
sky and earth
reason and dream
are things that do not belong together.

It is fairly chilling reading this, as so much of it seems true even now, so many years after it was written. In fact, in the UK, some might say that things have become rather worse, in the sense that teachers are more and more having to remain in control, unable to hand control to the children, since children have to be taught to meet prescribed outcomes. Children's interests and needs, their questions and theories, have little if any place in such a system. Even more chilling is that fact that this applies even to the very youngest children in our society. This is the challenge that all teachers must address.

The teacher as researcher

When I met Malaguzzi in 1992 I took brief notes in order to compile a report on my return. Here is what I said about rights, conditions and roles of teachers in Reggio Emilia at that time:

> The centres work as cooperatives. There is no head teacher or organiser. All staff work directly with children and parents. The cook and cleaning staff are included in all staff training and are seen as key personnel within the centre. All members of staff are called teachers, whether qualified or not. They are all aware of the learning and developmental needs of children and work in the same way. Training takes

place within the centres and is delivered by one of a team of 100 pedagogical coordinators employed by the region. These coordinators are
qualified teachers and each is responsible for between three and four
centres. Meetings take place weekly, in the evenings between 4 pm and
6 pm. Few children are still on the premises and a member of staff is
bought in to cover these meetings. Staff all work a 36-hour week and
have six hours of non-contact time, which means time for meetings,
study, documenting children's progress and more. The type of training
varies from coordinator to coordinator. We saw the following training
programmes on offer: for new staff, and including an induction into
early learning and, the organisation and routines of the day; music; the
particular needs of babies and more. The coordinators meet together
regularly. There are links with the University of Bologna.

It is interesting to note that, despite the undisputed quality of the provision
in Reggio Emilia, to this day there are no formal initial teaching training
programmes for teachers in either the scuole dell'infanzia or the nidi. People
with high school certificates or degrees may work as teachers, but all of them
are continually engaged in weekly sessions of professional development.
The focus of the sessions is primarily pedagogical. There is an interesting
dichotomy here between countries where there is an emphasis on initial
teacher training and Reggio, where ongoing professional development is
regarded as essential.

Research was and still is at the heart of Malaguzzi's project. Ongoing,
classroom-based research takes place in every centre, across centres,
nationally and internationally. We cited the small example of very young
children and their teachers researching the cherry tree close to their
infant-toddler centre. For many, the suggestion that this constitutes
research is laughable. But read on and perhaps you will come to see how
this makes sense.

In our society it is common to make a distinction between the teachers
working with children in classrooms, nurseries, preschools and infant-
toddler groups, and researchers carefully conducting and analysing research
in universities. For Malaguzzi and his followers, research is the everyday
activity that takes place in the classroom and is 'done' by teachers and
children.

Here is an example of how it works:

> During a discussion with some children it became clear that they were
> unsure of what the word 'crowd' meant to them. Did it just mean lots of
> people all in the same place? Or did it mean lots of people all going in
> the same direction? Could a group of children be called a crowd or did
> the word only apply to groups of adults?

In the spirit of being researchers, wanting the children to raise and know how to answer questions, the teachers working with them decided to take them out into the piazza during a busy time of day. There the children, with their teachers, watched the people, talked about them, commented on what they were doing and then returned to the preschool. To help them take this further the children were invited to work together to make a crowd of their own by drawing and cutting out figures and placing these in a box so that they were massed together. After much discussion children decided they could draw people looking straight ahead, in profile or from behind. They decided some should be men and some women, some old and some young, some adult and some children. A project started. Children drew one another, used the photocopier to enlarge or reduce figures, asked friends to pose, considered how to make a figure look as though it was moving. The figures were all pasted upright in a box and in this way the children had made their own version of a crowd. During the time of its making they also acted out being in crowds, made three-dimensional models of walking figures, sketched faces and talked.

What did the children learn from this? I would suggest that they developed a real understanding of what a crowd is. They learned that they needed to work with others in order to make the number of figures they needed for the final model to represent a crowd. They learned that photocopiers can enlarge and reduce images. They learned that thin paper would not stand upright. Perhaps they learned that a crowd might be a group of people all going to the same event – maybe a football match or an opera. Perhaps they learned that large groups of children can be called crowds. Can large groups of insects, animals or flowers be called a crowd?

And the teachers? What did they learn? They learned that in order for the children to understand a word or a concept they needed opportunities to explore and represent it in different ways using some of the hundred languages Malaguzzi talked of. So the children should be encouraged to look at a crowd, invited to work together to make their own crowd, encourage to carefully observe a crowd, helped to fashion crowds out of paper, clay (at a later stage) and physically in the piazza within the preschool. For the teachers, it was essential to listen to and observe the children so that they could follow each lead given. They may have learned that they needed to photograph, record and document the process in order for it to be shared with parents, carers and community and family members. They learned that they needed to be responsive in ensuring that they were able to resource children's chosen activities appropriately.

Here is another example, cited by Krechevsky and Stork (2000). It refers to a project on faces, in which five girls in a preschool in Reggio Emilia got involved with the support of their teachers:

The children, aged only aged 4–5, have already had experience of working with clay and are familiar with some of the skills and tools available and necessary. The teachers working with them are involved in a small piece of research which relates to the deciding which kinds of questions are likely to keep the children involved and interested in what they are doing. On the walls are images of facial features – enlarged noses or eyes, eyebrows and nostrils – and transcriptions of comments and questions raised by the children, together with examples of the work on faces they have already done. The children are taken out to look at faces in real life and in galleries and museums. They talk to the other children in their group about their work at the end of each day. The teachers meet daily and sometimes with teachers from other schools. They are documenting everything that happens and one of the things they record is the decision made by the group of five that the final goal of the project will be clay, graphic and verbal portraits of each child in the class. They decide that they have to all agree what is to be included: it must be a group decision.

What do the children and the teachers learn here? The children are working both individually and in collaboration. Malaguzzi reminds us that the development of intelligence grows together with the development of socialisation. In a group children can share and pool evidence and ideas, offer suggestions, take advice, physically and emotionally help one another, scaffold one another's learning, talk and listen. From what they have observed about group versus individual work, the teachers in Reggio have said that most effective group size in the scuole dell'infanzia is between two and six children. This explains why the work you see going on in the scuole dell'infanzia is usually group work.

The teachers in Reggio see themselves as theory builders. They build knowledge through their rigorous documentation of what children say and do. They are collectively engaged in posing questions and gathering data as they watch, listen, observe, document and interpret. It is different from academic research. Here theories about learning emerge from an analysis of daily practice; meanings are made and new questions and hypotheses arise as the teachers become not only researchers but also learners in their own right.

The teacher as documenter

We have seen that one of the voices teachers have is that of researcher. They are trained on a regular basis to be attentive to what children say and do and to pay attention and respond to this through their interactions, relationships, the resources they make available and support. One of the most vital parts of this is the documentation and recording of what takes place. For events to be analysed and considered they need to be recorded in some way, so that what is being done is transparent, shareable and useful to others.

What they are doing, in effect, is gathering evidence. You will remember Malaguzzi's thought that a teacher documenting what is happening is like an archaeologist.

It is important to note that this recording and documentation has little or nothing to do with ticking boxes, meeting pre-determined goals or passing tests. It is a very human way of gathering evidence about everyday events in the lives of the children and their teachers. Here are a few examples for you to consider:

> It has been raining and there is a puddle in the playground. The children are drawn to the water and they find some objects to stand on so that they can really see into the water. No one tells them not to get wet. No one warns them to be careful. Two teachers are with them and one has a camera. The other has a notebook. Emilia, learning over, notices her face reflected in the water. She tells her friends and they search for their images. Sarita says that she looks upside down. Giulio says it is like looking in the mirror. The teacher with the camera takes pictures and the one with the notebook records what the children are saying. When the children go indoors they want to keep talking about the water mirror, as Emilia calls it, and the teacher introduces the word 'reflection'. They talk about how funny the Italian word for upside down is: *sottosopra* (which means 'under above'). The episode develops into a small project with children drawing their own faces, their faces in a mirror, their faces distorted by ripples in a puddle; some of them begin to experiment with doing their images upside-down and their drawing become more cartoon like.

You will find other examples of documentation in the chapter about babies and toddlers.

The document panels on the walls contain the following:

- A series of photographs showing the children and what they are doing as they explore and talk about the puddle.
- The notes the teacher has made recording what she has heard the children say as they play. It is here that the word *sottosopra* (used by one of the teachers) first appears, together with the children's thoughts about what a funny word it is.
- The series of drawings the children made of their faces reflected in the puddle and reflected in mirrors.
- Some paintings the children have done of things as they are and things upside-down.
- A series of drawings the children made using pencils and inks to illustrate the effects of ripples in water. This came about when it rained for a second time and the children went out to place things in the puddles

that formed and then watched as the wind or their movements with sticks created ripples.
- The things the children said as they interpreted what was happening.

A different kind of documentation is the making of a video or film. This can be shown to parents and to children, and also be used by groups of teachers. It is part of the ongoing professional development of all teachers. In this example, what is being documented is not so much the development of individual children but an illustration of what a teacher did in response to a particular struggle she observed children having in using tools. It comes from an example cited in Edwards *et al.* (2011):

> Paola the teacher worked with a small group of 3 year olds exploring how to manipulate large lumps of clay. She felt it imperative to give the children some instruction about how to do this successfully so that they did not experience failure in their attempts. She began by giving each child a flat slab of clay which she had prepared in front of them, rolling it with a rolling pin and cutting the sides straight. Throughout the recorded session Paola offered individual children both tools and advice, intervened to help sort out a dispute about a tool, gave positive feedback, praise, suggestions and physical help. The children had cutting and rolling tools nearby. Paola thought that the children might want to try and give a sense of motion by folding the clay, but the children followed their own interests.

In more recent years documentation has been produced in the form of books, published by Reggio Children, which give accounts of children's projects, illustrated by photographs of the children at work, their drawings, paintings, models, maps, plans and designs. More than that, the conversations between children and adults are also recorded. They are delightful, informative, sometimes funny, often moving and always informative. But it is an expensive model, not easily replicated in less fortunate places.

It is important to remember that documentation here is part of the whole process of pedagogy. The way in which learning takes place is through the this cycle of a long-term *progettazione*, where every step is recorded, considered, discussed, responded to and changes made, which may constitute the second step and so on.

In the UK we keep records of progress, but these are primarily a record of each child's progress on the road to some predetermined goal or target. We do share these records with parents, but do not really use the process of documentation as part of our pedagogy. In Reggio, with its history rooted in the community, its genesis in the activities of women and others fighting for secular and high-quality early years education, it is a standard part of classroom practice.

Lillian Katz, educationalist, researcher and friend of Reggio, says that this documentation is one of the most significant aspects raising and maintaining the quality of the services. She argues that it works in several ways. When the children see what they have done or are still doing valued, recorded and displayed for all to see, they feel pleased with their own achievements. But they also see what their peers have done and are doing and can learn from that. Panels of documentation are as embedded in each preschool as are easels, books and toys. Children, parents, teachers and visitors examine and read these as part of everyday life. Malaguzzi, watching and listening as the children scan the panels displaying their work, believed that they become 'more curious, interested and confident as they contemplate the meaning of what they have achieved' (cited in Katz and Cesarone 1994). They get a sense that their work, their efforts, have been recognised, appreciated and respected. And as the children almost always work in small groups, they are working with others, so it is a celebration of negotiation and collaboration, of sharing and learning together.

One of Malaguzzi's oft-stated principles is *transparency*. For him, the schools were public spaces open to those in the local community. They are publicly funded and where the future of the community is being determined through the education of the children. Working closely with parents is more than just words and the occasional meeting. It is a vital ingredient in the pedagogy of relationships. When the parents see what the children have been doing they gain some idea of just what the children – their children and the children of their friends and neighbours – are capable of. If you have seen the artwork the children produce in the scuole dell'infanzia and the nidi and read what the children say, you begin to see how important high expectations are. Malaguzzi's words again:

> documentation introduces parents to a quality of knowing that tangibly changes their expectations. They re-examine their assumptions about their parenting roles and their views about the experience their children are living and take a new and more inquisitive approach toward the whole school experience.
>
> (Katz 1994)

Guido Giarelli is the parent of a child at the *Fiastri* preschool. This is what he said about the work of children, including his own child, displayed in the book *Il Futuro e una Bella Giornata*. He is an anthropologist and was deeply moved by the children's thinking about the future:

> The future becomes object, person, animate or inanimate being – it's a mountain where 'there's a road with a little man who can only go up' (Giorgia), 'it's a tunnel 'cause all the years pass through it' (Elena),

'perhaps he lives underground and comes out of the little holes in the ground that are closed with corks' (Omnia), 'it's like the air ... it moves all around the sky' (Dario), 'it's a round, coloured ball and inside there are all the shapes' (Elena), 'It's inside us, in our heads' (Christian) and 'it's a little voice inside us that knows lots of things, it knows what it's got to do!' (Elena).

(The children of the Fiastri and Rodari preschools, 2010)

The teacher as scaffolder

Hopefully you remember that one of the thinkers who most influenced Malaguzzi was Vygotsky, and one of the most significant things Vygotsky talked about was how important it was for any teacher to be able to capture that moment where it is possible for the child to take the next step toward learning. Vygotsky talked of the *zone of proximal development*, which was the notional gap between what the child could do alone and what the child might do with help. It is the step between what the child is observed to be able to do unassisted and what the child could do potentially. Malaguzzi talks of this as the distance between the levels of capacities expressed by children and their levels of potential development, attainable with the help of adults or more advanced contemporaries.

This is really important but difficult to grasp, because the gap is not something visible or real, but something notional. Malaguzzi talks of 'circularity' and what he means is that the teacher's aim is to set up a situation where the child can almost see what the adult already sees. The gap is small and if the adult provides carefully matched help or support the child will be able to leap over the gap. Bruner, elaborating on Vygotsky's ideas, used the term 'scaffolding' to explain what it is the adult can do to help the child make this leap. He borrowed the term 'scaffold' from building and used it to illustrate the idea of something that supports an existing structure until work is complete and the building can stand without it. Thus the adult provides the support to allow the child to be able to do something without help. Here are some simple examples:

Dario is starting to walk. He wants to get from the settee, which he is holding onto, to the table, but that means taking several steps without support. His mum puts out her hand but at a distance, which requires him to take one step without support before he reaches it. She assessed what she thought he could do without help and provided the physical help (the small step) to enable him to do this.

Serena is making something out of clay and has trouble making her three-dimensional figure stand. The atelierista asks her, 'Do you need something to help you make that stay up?' She nods. So the teacher hands her a thick wooden stick. The little girl examines it and then inserts it in the centre of her figure. Delighted that it works she claps her hands in glee. The teacher decides that the scaffold she has offered can be extended to offering some additional and specific vocabulary. She says: 'That piece of wood gave you something strong enough to hold the weight of all that clay. It is a support'.

Vea Vecchi, who was, for many years, the atelierista at the Diana school, is very clear about their decision to talk of 'language' where we might say 'discipline'. So mathematics, science, history, art, music, writing, acting and mime are all languages. Each has its own grammar, but all have developed in order to communicate. The hundred languages are the communicative possibilities with which our species – human beings – are genetically endowed. The assumption is that learning often involves several languages interacting together. Here are some small examples. In each case try and work out what languages the children are using:

> Javelle, drawing people, always started with the feet. He was the only child in his class to do that and, when I asked him why, he stood up to illustrate his answer, 'See, they have to be first to make sure the person is on the ground. Then I can make the legs and then the body and then the head'. I asked, 'What if you want to draw someone sitting down?' He sat down to try it out and replied, 'Feet still on the ground so same place'. He was 5 at the time.

> In a later chapter in this book you will find a little girl who dances what she thinks a cell would be like.

> Alice, aged 4, found some violets flowering early, in a sheltered place by a low wall. The next day a cold wind was blowing so she went out to make a shelter for them using dry leaves.

> A 2-year-old boy found a rose lying on the ground and put it on the wall, saying that it was sleeping.

> A group of children adopted a small tree in the garden of the school, in the courtyard. They tended it. One day they decided to make clay birds to live in the tree and described the tree as being lonely so the birds will provide company for it.
>
> (Some of these last examples are from personal experience and the others are drawn from the work at Via Vecchi)

We could call this way of thinking interdisciplinary or transdisciplinary – the way in which human beings use every means available to them in order to understand something more clearly. In the Reggio system care is taken that children are introduced into new ways of expressing and re-expressing their developing thoughts and ideas. They look, listen, feel, describe, discuss, question, raise theories, seek help, explore with their hands or feet or body, measure with found objects or measuring devices, use pens or pencils or markers of paint to make a representation, use cut-out paper or found things to make a symbolic representation, use clay or other materials to make a three dimensional representation and involve others in dancing or acting or performing an idea. They dress up, make and put on masks and try out different voices. They use rhyme, invent words and bring in pet words from home. They explore sounds and rhythms, tone and pitch. They see the influence of light and shade and dark, of inside or out, of position, surroundings, structures and style. The list is almost endless.

Leibnitz, a famous mathematician and philosopher, and something of a linguist, believed that mathematics was the music of thought. He famously said, 'When God sang, he sang in algebra' (Steiner 2004: 46). The children in Reggio seem to sing in all of their hundred languages.

The teacher as initiator and partner

We have looked at the teacher as researcher and documenter. The skills and languages required for these roles are many, including acute listening and observation, careful analysis, accurate recording, the application of peda-gogical thinking and communicating clearly with different audiences. The teacher as initiator and partner requires these same languages, but also those of persuasion, argument, negotiation, collaboration, sharing and listening. Some examples of teachers in the roles will make this clear:

> Every year in May children and adults in the scuole dell'infanzia and nidi come together in a very public demonstration of how much they love and value their city. Three sites in the city are transformed for one day by what the children and their teachers bring and do. What they bring and do relates to what they have been doing at their centres.

> At the *Picasso infant–toddler* centre the staff initiated what they called compositional research. They defined compositions as ensembles of small objects – natural and made things, all small, of different colours and materials, textures and densities. The children explored and handled the objects and played with them, and began to sort them, group them, build with them, work collaboratively in pairs or small groups. Rebecca said, 'It's a tower with windows … I'm putting the king and queen inside it'. Silvia broke a lump of clay into small pieces, which she arranged horizontally in word-like patterns and said, 'I'm writing. I'm making

letters'. Some of the children played at the light table where the made scenes – landscapes built of objects of different qualities, densities and consistencies. After or during their play the children raised questions. The question raised by the teachers was the extent to which the materials they had provided had started or stimulated the whole thing, and could they launch it back to give the children control. They had initiated a project rather than following the lead given by the children. Their solution was brilliant. They showed the children slides of the work done by some of them and, as they had expected, this sharing of the work started discussion that led to planning and the project changed direction – this time led by the children.

The role of the teachers is most often to be responsible for finding, organising and offering the resources in response to what the children are doing. Sometimes – as here – the teacher becomes the initiator. We find other examples where the teacher tells or reads a story to a group, takes the children on an outing, finds something of beauty or interest to share or plays music to the children. Within such events the interest of one or two children will be captured and they will continue to follow that up, often joined by others who catch the fever of excitement generated. What is essential in either case is that the teacher engages in sharing activities with the children, sometimes leading, sometimes following, always scaffolding learning and always listening.

The teacher as advocate

From the earliest days of the development of the preschool programmes in Reggio, taking the message out into the community and being able and willing to talk about what was being done and why has been essential to the success of the venture. You will remember Malaguzzi taking the children and classrooms out into the city squares to show what the children were doing and learning. The public face of the preschools has always been important. We have just seen what happens each May as the children and their teachers take over the public spaces of *Via Farini, Vicolo Travelli* and the city park in Reggio Emilia to showcase their art, music, dance and theatre – everything they do using their hundred languages. When the municipality was in discussion with Malaguzzi about the development and future of preschools, many companies and factories started to donate waste and left-over materials to the new preschools to facilitate children's graphic development. They were given screeds of paper, cartons, cotton reels, buttons, sequins, lace, fabric off-cuts, bits of wood and more. Then, in 1996, *Remida*, a creative recycling centre, was born. It is still in existence today, its aim being to ensure that creativity can be nourished through traditional art materials, but also through the use of found, waste, natural and left-over materials. *Gunther Kress* (1997) talks about children making objects, statements and even metaphors from what is 'at hand'. In this way, objects are recycled and those involved are developing a purposeful living ecology around waste and sustainability and respect for the object, the human and the environment. *Remida Day* has become an annual celebration.

The teacher as cultural co-constructor and civic leader

The children and adults in the scuola dell'infanzia or nido share and make a culture together within the framework of that of the wider community. Culture is a system of agreed values and principles, ideas and artefacts. We have touched on how the history of the region affected those who started the movement. Malaguzzi, you will remember, was a passionate anti-fascist and valued highly the rights of women to work and have quality care and education for their children, and the rights of the children to a secular education that would allow them to question and go beyond the roles expected of their previous generations. They were fortunate to share many of the cultural values of their region and municipality. So the preschool movement started in a climate that was essentially political, seeing education as a vital force in the liberation of the poor and viewing children as competent, questioning, and entitled.

What takes place in each preschool or infant-toddler centre is that something happens – a child brings in something from home or says something that catches the attention of an adult and the cycle begins. Building on a child's interest or a cultural tool introduced by an adult starts the educational process of questioning, listening, exploring, inventing, discussing, making, evaluating, sharing and reflecting. During the process culture is created.

A sublime example is the creation of a new curtain for the baroque theatre in Reggio Emilia, which involved the children visiting the theatre, discussing and designing the curtain, working, as always, in collaboration with one another and with their teachers, and then using computer technology to make the curtain. The theatre is a cultural space in the small town, which the children and their families visit. The old curtain – a cultural artefact – had been made by *Alfonso Chierici* and was regarded and valued as part of the history of the town. When it was worn out the theatre management decided to invite the children from the Diana Preschool to design and make a new one. The process of doing this was prolonged and, in the spirit of all things to do with Reggio and its children, collaborative, educational and ultimately beautiful. The whole of the next chapter is devoted to the making of the curtain, since it illustrates perfectly the hundred languages of children and the corresponding responses of teachers.

Looking back, looking ahead

In this chapter we have looked at what the teachers do in response to the hundred languages of children. We see them as listeners, initiators, partners, responders, researchers and advocates. In the next chapter we study in detail one of the most ambitious and public progettazione: the design of the theatre curtain. Here we see the dance between the teachers and children as they work together, listen and respond to one another, learn together and enjoy.

Chapter 7

The story of the theatre curtain

> I will not hide from you how much hope we invested in the introduction of the atelier. We knew it would be impossible to ask for anything more. Yet if we could have done so, we would have gone further still by creating a new type of school typology with a new school made entirely of laboratories similar to the atelier. We would have constructed a new type of school made of space where the hands of children could be active for 'messing about' ... With no possibility of boredom, hands and minds would engage each other with great, liberating merriment in the way ordained by biology and evolution.
>
> (Malaguzzi in Edwards *et al.* 2011: 49)

In the previous two chapters we have looked at the hundred languages used by children and considered how this requires a hundred responses from their teachers. To illustrate this I am going to tell you the story of what happened when *Elio Canova*, the president of *I Teatri Consortium* in Reggio Emilia, had a brainwave. One of the two curtains in the theatre was damaged and needed to be repaired and restored. Canova, a passionate supporter of the work of Reggio Children, had the inspired idea of asking the children at the Scuola Diana to design a curtain. He knew that this was something real, relevant and culturally significant. The children knew the theatre, went there with their families and others, and here was a magnificent opportunity for them to use their hundred languages to produce something real, beautiful, useful and visible for their own community.

Sandra Piccini, Commissioner for Culture and Education for the municipality, celebrates the long history of the city's involvement with young children, but believes that children anywhere could become engaged in something similar to the making of the theatre curtain. The role of civic leader, in this context, refers to the role of making manifest why preschool education is important to all of society and how it is that the care and learning of young children is the responsibility of the whole community. There is very little sense of this happening in the UK, but it is evident in

Reggio, where community involvement has been and remains a vital ingredient in the life of the city. I think this may be true for places that establish and maintain a dialogue with children. In London there is the Unicorn Theatre, set on the south bank of the river, a place that has long valued young children, theatre, narrative, the arts and culture. When you visit you often find exhibitions of children's artwork on display there – but let us carry on with the story.

You will remember how Malaguzzi set about spreading word of his vision for early years education at the beginning of the project. In doing this he ensured that the preschools became public spaces, just like theatres. You will also have read about how the city itself becomes a sort of giant theatre at least once a year, when the children and their teachers and families take to the streets to celebrate children and their learning.

You should know that this wonderful city now has 140,000 inhabitants and is growing at a very rapid rate. Contrary to popular belief, it is now a culturally and linguistically diverse society with over a hundred different ethnic groups represented. The schools and the theatres – and the streets, squares and parks – belong to everyone.

This chapter is based on the wonderful work of Vea Vecchi, atelierista at the Scuola Diana and now a consultant for Reggio Children. Her excellent *Theater Curtain: the Ring of Transformations*, published by Reggio Children, is an example of documentation made into a book (2002).

NOTE: In this chapter, I highlight what the teachers do using a different font. This is to make it easy for you, as the reader, to see where the teacher is initiator, where follower and where collaborator.

The story begins: first steps, first marks, first ideas

Those planning the project realised that it had to start as many of the projects do, with a hands-on experience, in this case with a visit to the theatre. It was clear that the project would involve some issues including a recognition that the techniques used had to be economical and and simple in the light of the limited budget; the curtain would have to conform to safety requirements and be fire retardant; the actual enormous size of the curtain meant that it would not be possible for the children to work on the final version; decisions would have to be made about where to work, who could be involved and whether some children would have to be selected for the final stages.

1   The first step then was a visit to the theatre, which was a place not unfamiliar to them, but in this case they were going to be really looking at it with fresh eyes. The building itself is impressive with statues along the front, a portico below the statues, arches, windows of different shapes and sizes, reliefs and plaques on the walls and gardens.

The children walked and looked and talked and the teachers, alongside them, wrote down what they said. Here are some of their ideas:

It's really big! It has lots of columns and a whole lot of windows.
I don't know who lives there.
They put statues on the roof so the theatre would become more important.
Maybe the statues are of the dead people who built it.
There's probably the name and 1800 written on them.

You can see the hypotheses children are making as they look and think.

2   The children explored the space, running through the portico, climbing on the steps, running in and out of the columns, stroking the columns in a made up repeated game. They go in and out, round and round, up and down.

3   Then the children were asked by the teachers to make a graphic representation of the building from the outside. These, like many of the drawing that emerge from the Reggio children are remarkable in their attention to detail, sense of pattern and observation of architectural features. The teachers, in their comments on these initial drawings, say that 'drawing requires moments of concentration and attention' so the relationship between different things is noticed. From the front the columns are in a straight line, with gaps between, above them are shuttered windows, above these are decorative plaques on the wall and above again are the statues. From the side it is more difficult to see and place the statues. From the back there are no statues visible, but a pitched roof appears.

4   Then the children were taken inside where there are tiers with columns, gold everywhere, a wonderful domed and painted ceiling and more. Here are what some of the children said:

Wow! It looks like the theatre of heaven.
Look at that chandelier! It's a light with white diamonds inside it!
There's a round thing like a world that has people painted on it who are flying and horses with wings, then there are some woods, some lakes and the sky with clouds.
Then there's a thousand lights – yellow, green and red and when the show starts they go off and everything gets dark.

The teachers note that the children become more still and less talkative, gazing upwards in wonderment. Then they suggest to the children that they follow the semi-circular perimeter of the stalls, running their fingers along the wall as they do so. Then they hear the children using metaphor and simile:

It's made like an arch.
It's like half an egg.

At this point the children know nothing about the proposal for them to design the curtain for this theatre. For them it is one of the lovely excursions they regularly enjoy. But when the children start to look at the existing curtain and talk about what it represents, the teachers ask them what they think of the idea of designing a new curtain. Here are some of their responses:

I don't think we could do it because it would take too long, at least eleven days.

Look, something that big can hold the ideas of all the kids. Not just one idea but lots of ideas.

I guess somebody better go up on the stage and measure it.

You will have guessed that they decide to measure the width of the curtain using their bodies. They count the number of footsteps and the number of times their open arms are used. The teachers, attentive as ever, notice that some anxiety about the size is creeping into the children's thoughts, so they decide to tell the children at this point that what they will do is make the design smaller than the final curtain and then use special techniques to enlarge it.

The last step of this initial visit is for the children to look at, explore and draw the inside of the theatre – an immensely difficult task since the inside is so complex.

Back at school: moving on

1   The first thing the teachers did on the return to the school was to get the children to physically redraw, using gross motor movements – their estimate of the width of the curtain in the central square – the piazza. This was the largest open space in the school. The children again paced out or used wide open-arm counts, and then a meter stick. Although the children would initially be working on a smaller scale, some notional idea of the approximate dimensions needed to be referred back to.

2   The teachers then asked the children for their thoughts on the theatre and the visit. Here are some things the children said:

Maybe they asked us to make a new curtain because they think we're really good at it.

I think it's because our school is the closest to the theatre.

As always the teachers listened respectfully to what the children were saying and noticed that one of the things that most impressed children were the elaborately patterned pieces of highly gilded stucco work all over the walls and ceiling. The children called these 'rubber stamps', no doubt in reference to rubber stamps they had at home. They immediately set out to make their own designs for rubber stamps. In the theatre these took many forms – flowers, leaves, ducks, birds and tendrils. The children's designs included all of these but also hearts, snakes and a wide range of patterns. There were lines, zigzags, dots and spirals. A world of line and colour.

Over the next few days all the children, in small groups, visited the theatre. Some of them visited the non-public areas so they could see the device for lowering the curtain or the large electrical board covered in cables and switches, and some of the children made elaborate drawings, like diagrams, of these devices.

Beautiful shapes, happy things, the sun and moon and stars

1   When the teachers asked what would be suitable images to put on a theatre curtain, the children did not hesitate. They wanted beautiful things, things to make people feel happy, things that would be fun to draw, that that would create a feeling of peace. They insisted that scorpions, snakes and beetles could not be included, but other little creatures like dragonflies and pretty grasshoppers could. The teachers concluded that the children were thinking about representing the things they liked, made them happy and were important and interesting. But they also remembered and made a note of the fact that the children had been very interested in insects in the spring and felt that some of this was influencing their choices.

2   So the drawing began. The children could use a range of resources for this. Remember that they have had much experience in this area and are used to having the support of the atelierista. They could draw their plants, creatures or the sun from real observation, through exploring images in books, memory or invention. But keen that the children should retain a sense of the things they were drawing being alive, the teachers tried to embed in the process some discussion and investigation of scientific processes relating to how plants grow, what energy is and so on: they call this the 'pulsing of life'.

Between biology and magic: transformations and change

The children began to draw and as they drew they talked, began to create narratives and to look at what the other children were doing. A wonderful moment – and one that changed the whole project – was when Giovanni said, 'My plant is transforming, it's in a phase of transformation,' and, after a while, went on, 'Why don't we do it so that the things we draw get transformed into other things?'

Vea Vecchi calls moments like this in the life of the scuole dell'infanzia generative moments, where one thing steers the work in a particular direction. I guess we might call it a light bulb moment. But Vecchi's analysis of where Giovanni's idea came from is fascinating. She says that the children themselves are growing, and growing means change and transformation. As children they also watch a lot on television and in films where magical transformations are common and through these media very visible. They then play out transformations in school, at home, in the piazza and parks. For Vecchi transformations and metamorphosis are processes somewhere between biology (natural physical growth and change) and magic (fantastical change).

So the one of the teachers, Paola, started asking the children what they thought of Giovanni's idea. The children were articulate and thoughtful in their responses. All liked the idea of transformations but they all agreed that the subject – the thing to be transformed – had to be the one to decide whether to be transformed or not. They also agreed that the subject should be allowed to return to its original state.

Here the teachers really show how respectful they are of children's ownership of the processes of drawing and making. Since the subject has the right to be changed into something else and back again, each child must have access to two sheets of paper – one for the unchanged subject and one for the transformation. Should the subject want to go back to its original state, there it is, on the first sheet of paper.

The children have access to soft pencils, coloured pencils, black markers and coloured marks with thin or thick tips. They have a choice of A4 or A3 paper, as well as large sheets of patterned paper. They also have access to erasers, which they love. The erasers are liberating in that they allow the child to erase mistakes easily and to successfully change the original.

NOTE: This paragraph is in the teachers' font, because it is the teachers who offer the resources from which the children can chose.

> The transformations begin. Some children find it easier than others. Some seem to make unrelated doodles beside their original drawing, whilst others clearly change or transform some aspect of the original. As the children draw they offer monologues and narratives. Giovanni drew a wonderful grasshopper and his transformation was to lengthen the grasshopper's legs. He said, 'When the grasshopper is transformed he always has a little bit of leg ...'

> Giorgio drew the sun and a leaf and said, 'When I made the transformation of the sun, I was thinking about its energy and I made the shapes of energy. But when I made the plant I was thinking about its energy that makes it grow with its roots, with water and light.'

Which shall I choose: computer or paper? Creating the composition

After time spent making lots of drawings, the children were asked to select the ones they would like to see become part of the curtain. Once they had chosen, these needed to be made into one composition and this, as you can imagine, was a tricky part of the process. The teachers decided that there were two alternatives for the children:

- The tried and tested process of cutting out the chosen drawing and then set about placing them and moving them around on a larger sheet of paper to make the composition
- The other using the computers by scanning in the drawings to be viewed on the screen. The objects can then be manipulated by being enlarged or rotated and placed in different positions.

The teachers, aware of the existing and potential role of the digital revolution in the lives of coming generations decided that the children needed to become familiar with what was possible using computers. They offered the children two programmes to use and the children, not surprisingly, learned very quickly how to use them. What the teachers wanted to do was to observe carefully what the children did as they played with the programmes on the computers. They were looking to see what methods the children used and this process of observation and documentation is a basic, fundamental and very important part of Malaguzzi's thinking about pedagogy. They were observing both individual and group strategies, and keeping detailed notes on what they were doing.

The children, using the computer, stressed the images – in other words they used the computer to take the image to its limits by enlarging or shrinking it, and noticing what happened. Here are some of their comments:

It is getting skinnier and skinnier, it disappeared!

Look at this grasshopper. It's a monster!

At this stage the children are not very interested in making multiple images, although they will come back to this later in the process. The teachers notice and comment on the fact that children, at the computers, work in silence, which is unusual for Reggio. But they do mimic what they notice by pulling faces and exclamations of horror or glee. They also notice that the children using the computer are happy for images to overlap, whereas using paper they avoid this.

As the children's physical prowess on the computers improve, they begin to make up narratives about what they are doing. Some children work using paper, cutting and sticking to make a variety of compositions.

Some children use a digital camera. Some children move from computer to paper to digital camera and back again: evidence of children using new and known languages as part of their expressive vocabulary. And the teachers, observing and documenting all the time, develop and extend their languages in response.

At this point the teachers decided to ask the children to evaluate the different techniques they had been using. This invitation to reflect on your own learning is another feature of the pedagogy operating in Reggio. Here is what some of them said:

> The computer is stronger: you can make them bigger or smaller and you can make them appear and then appear again; you can change it and make the designs you want.

> I didn't discover anything with the computer. With the sheets of paper I moved the drawings around, one at the bottom, one at the top, one here, on there.

The role of narrative: growing into a linked image

At this time there began to be a feeling that people – children and adults – were losing their way. The images being manipulated still seemed to be isolated and separate, rather than forming a meaningful whole new composition. To help resolve this problem the children were invited to make up stories about the elements to link them into a single narrative.

Nearly there: dancing Mimi's cell

The final stages of making the curtain involve a number of activities and decisions. The children get involved in the process of enlarging their images on to sheets of acetate using an overhead projector. By now, a smaller number of children are involved in the work and these consist of two groups each of three children, and they became a boys' group and a girls' group. The children are selected on the basis of having been very interested in the project, the strategies they have demonstrated and their competencies. The teachers are keen that there should be a real mix of strategies and competencies in each group.

The children have to reach agreement about which of the two final images should be selected to become the curtain. Not surprisingly each group argues for their own image and it is only the generosity and honesty of one of the girls after a very lively discussion that allows the final decision to be made. The image made by the boys is the one chosen.

You can read more about the finished versions and see wonderful pictures of the whole process in Vecchi's book (2011), which you will find listed in the bibliography at the end of this book.

As is customary at the Diana scuola dell'infanzia, the children and their teachers share what has been happening with all the other children in the class and get their support for the choice that has been made.

The last stage involves the six children going to paint the real pattern onto a plastic sheet. There is no space to do this in the school and the theatre offer the group the use of their painter's loft. Two to three children and their teachers spend 20 days in the loft working on the design. When the children have completed their work, the design will be digitised and printed onto the fabric.

As the children work, painting on the acetate sheet placed on top of the enlarged black and white design they have agreed on, they continue to talk and look and move around. The teachers have set out a wide range of paint colours and brushes and they place a stepladder in the loft so that the children can look down on their work. The teachers suggest they do this every so often. Sometimes the children work close together, enjoying the intimacy and opportunity to chat. Sometimes they call one another over for an opinion, advice or physical help. As they gain confidence their brush strokes become bolder and purposeful. They are reinterpreted as they look and respond to what they see.

The teachers let them have a digital camera to use as they please and to provide a record of what takes place. When the children are tired they stop to dance or run around. The loft is big enough for groups of children from their class to come and work on their own projects.

Then something amazing happens. The painting is almost finished when Leonardo asks, 'Why don't we put in some cells that come from outer space? And then they can decide what shape they want to be?' How in the spirit of the whole project this idea is: some natural form that can choose its own shape and, presumably, its own transformation. There is a lot of discussion about what a cell looks like and one child suggests looking in a book, another says he does not want to do that because he has a picture of cells in his mind. At this point a little girl called Mimi gets up and starts moving around in a spontaneous dance whilst the others draw their ideas of cells. Then she sits down and Giovanni gets up to dance and this is what he says:

> I'm dancing Mimi's cell ... look, I'm, following her drawing with my body ... I'm copying it by dancing. I'm copying her drawing with a dance, and before she was dancing my cell.

For me this is the most wonderful description of just how these privileged children have learned to use their range of languages in order to communicate their thoughts and feelings with others.

So the children completed their design, including cells, and an informal preview of the curtain in situ is arranged for all the children who participated and their families. Soon after the children went to the theatre to see a ballet performance where they saw their curtain lowered and raised.

Looking back, looking ahead

This chapter has been devoted to describing one project carried out in one scuola dell'infanzia in Reggio Emilia. It has been described in detail because it is such an amazing example of the ongoing and equal dialogue between the children and their teachers. The respect they have for one another is evident. Each group is aware of their roles in the dialogue – the teachers to sometimes initiate, but always to then follow the leads given by the children. This means really attentive listening, looking, analysing and thinking and also documenting. So one thing leads on to another. It is also a perfect example of how all of the children's languages – actual and potential – are considered and, again, valued and respected. So when Mimi dances a cell no one tells her that she cannot, or that cells do not dance. They take her expression very seriously. It is her hypothesis that you can show what a cell looks like through music.

In the next chapter we turn our attention to the youngest children and to Malaguzzi's thoughts about what they needed in order to flourish and learn.

Chapter 8

Responding to the needs of babies and toddlers

> To be sure, our schools are the most visible object of our work. I believe they give multiple perceptions and messages. They have decades of experience behind them, and have known three generations of teachers. Each infant-toddler centre and each preschool has its own past and evolution, its own layers of experience, and its peculiar mix of styles and cultural levels. There has never been, on our part, any desire to make them all alike.
>
> (Malaguzzi in Edwards *et al.* 2011: 330–1)

The first asilo nido, or infant-toddler centre, came into being in 1971, just one year before a new national law in Italy that required municipalities to provide care for children from about 4 months to 3 years of age came into effect. This law was a victory particularly for all the women, who had spent ten years struggling to assert their rights to be workers and students whilst their very young children were well cared for. In this chapter we will look at the dilemmas that faced Malaguzzi and his colleagues, and the decisions they made and why. You will be familiar by now with the approach of examining all of this in tune with the context and the culture.

In this chapter we look at how the provision came about, how important the environment is as a partner in the learning process and two crucial issues: the role of the atelier and the prevailing practices of active listening and pedagogical documentation.

The prevailing ethos: a delicate question

There are still people who will argue that babies and toddlers should not be put into any form of group care, but should be at home with their mothers or another primary caregiver. So it is hardly surprising that, not just in Reggio Emilia, not just in Italy, but further afield, it was argued and largely accepted that the mother-baby dyad was essential to the baby's development and to the family as a whole. To support this argument, the views and writings of *John Bowlby* and *Rene Spitz*, which had been rediscovered after the Second

World War, were cited. In Italy the Catholic Church added its voice, stating that the resulting breakdown of the family, inevitable if the child was put into group care, would give rise to unnamed dire and dreadful consequences. Raising the issue of providing education for very young children was therefore a delicate question that needed addressing.

Reggio Emilia had, by this time, gathered a body of evidence about the success of the scuole dell'infanzia, but this was clearly not enough in itself. Many in the community of Reggio accepted there was urgent need to provide group care for babies and toddlers, but who should do it, how it should be done and how the vital family relationships could be fostered even if a child was put in group care were the questions to be answered. The needs of younger children are somewhat different from those of older children so, although much could be learnt from the experience of the scuole dell'infanzia, new ways of operating needed to be explored.

Alongside the women agitating for quality care for their babies and toddlers was Malaguzzi, as intent on providing for these young children as he had been for their older siblings and friends. Just as he had led the battle for the scuole dell'infanzia, so he became one of the leaders of the new movement for nidi. Malaguzzi, together with people in the community and others, began to identify the particular needs and possible solutions for these, the youngest members of the community.

A welcoming space to reflect layers of culture

If you were asked what you think are the particular needs of young children what would you say? Here are the answers given first by a group of mothers in Camden in London and then a group of mothers in Reggio:

The Camden responses:

- Babies need, more than anything else, to be loved.
- They need to be kept safe.
- They need to have one particular care worker.
- They need to be in small groups.
- They need to be able to be fed, to sleep, to be changed, to be kept warm and to be cuddled.

The Reggio responses:

- They need to be helped to make the transition from being at home with the mother to being in the nido, and this will take a long time.
- They need to have spaces to belong to and to explore.
- They need to have lots of interesting and beautiful things to look at, and touch, smell and explore.
- They need to form relationships with the people they encounter.

- They need to have their family and their experience, culture and language welcomed.

I found this revealing because the expectations of the mothers in Reggio are so much higher than those of the Camden mothers. I attribute this to all the work Malaguzzi has done over years. There is an awareness of the rights of babies and toddlers to quality care and education there which is certainly less evident in the response from the mothers in London.

Bruner, on one of his many visits to Reggio, said, 'An infant-toddler centre, a school, is a special type of space where human beings are invited to develop their minds, attitudes, their sensitivity and their sense of belonging to a wider community'. The researcher *Colwyn Trevarthen*, said 'Infants under one year, who have no language, communicate much more powerfully and constructively with receptive adults than psychological science of rational processes has expected ... they rapidly develop skilful capacities for regulating intimate encounters with humour, teasing, and moral evaluations of different persons' (2011: 176). Malaguzzi himself had an absolute belief in the curiosity and competence of babies, born into a world with other people in it, where he said that 'the art of sympathetic and creative two-way communication is essential for "intent participation learning" at every stage of teaching, from kindergarten to university' (2012: 175–6). The term 'intent participation' was first used by Barbara Rogoff and her colleagues, and it meant what happens when the teacher pays absolute attention to what children are interested in and uses that as the basis for possibly intervening to take learning forward, offer help, support or resources or merely document. This is the essence of what good teachers of the babies, toddlers and older children do.

The needs of babies and toddlers are particular and touch on some deeply held beliefs about what is best for them, what they are capable of and who should care for them. The Camden mothers were concerned with safety and bonding, Bruner with their capacities to become members of wider communities, Trevarthen with the opportunities for them to be creative and competent from very early on and Malaguzzi with the importance of the social in their learning and development.

These very young children do share some things with older ones in terms of how much more competent they are than they are often given credit for, and for just how social and communicative they are. Like older children they are little researchers, constantly seeking to make sense of their world, exploring it with all available means and expressing their feelings and thoughts as they do so. Babies arrive with no spoken language, unable to care for their physical needs, yet they demonstrate that they react to the feelings of others, communicate with them, discriminate between sounds, show preferences and appear to follow a self-directed programme of development, which is related to the growth of their body and brain. At the risk of being repetitive, it is worth saying again that they do this best in interactions with others.

Designing a nido

When considering the design of the proposed nidi, Malaguzzi and his fellow planners followed the principle of creating an amiable school and one where children, teachers and family members will feel at home, welcomed and valued. You will remember that we talked of an amiable school in an earlier chapter. Leaving your baby in the care of others is a deeply emotional thing to do, and the mother must immediately get a sense of a place designed specifically for her child, where her child will be treated as an important, thinking, sensitive, creative, competent, unique and loved being. Another principle to be followed was that the nido must be overtly integrated into the community, welcoming and open to parents, teachers, children and visitors. The third key principle was that the building should be designed to facilitate real, working, equal partnerships with all involved. This feature meant that there should be dedicated space for the teachers to document all that happened so that it was visible, accessible and meaningful to parents and family members. It also meant that there needed to be spaces for people to meet, talk and share.

In her book, Vecchi (2002) talks to *Paolo Cavazzoni, Maddalena Tedeschi*, both pedagogisti, and *Tullio Zini*, an architect who designed many of the Reggio scuole dell'infanzia. They talk about what they can build on from their original designs and the experience of having seen the children using them. They know that they must take account of the fact that the children in the nidi will be much smaller, more dependent, less mobile to start with, but still thinking, learning, curious and communicative beings. One of the main considerations is how such small children will perceive, move around and inhabit any given space, and what they will do with the resources provided. You can see how everything they are thinking about relates to their view of childhood and teaching and learning, or pedagogy. Their starting point is Malaguzzi's – that of a pedagogy of relationships with its implications for creating spaces with strong connections to each other, so there is no separation from one kind of learning or experience and another. There is to be no space between playing and learning, kitchen and classroom, inside and outside. Learning takes place everywhere, through every interaction and in hundreds of different ways.

Like the scuole dell'infanzia, the nidi are built to include a very welcoming entrance. Beyond that there are differently sized spaces that implicitly refute the oft-stated idea that small children prefer to be in small spaces. The designers believe that tall spaces, for example, offer new ways of looking. A staircase between one floor and another offers possibilities of looking down or up or through. There must be a community space that can hold lots of people, where adults and children can be together. The designers recognise that the use of smaller spaces may be good for controlling children, but they want children to be able to look at things from different points of view. Perhaps you will be struck, as I was, by the lack of discussion of health and safety.

Tullio, the architect, talked of how he wanted to incorporate in his planning aspects that might be regarded as being part of the feminine world; what he meant by that is the world of women's culture, which he believes pays attention to details. In all the nidi you will see fresh flowers, soft fabrics, subtle colours, plants growing indoors and out and things that will be familiar to the some children. His aim is to create simple, basic landscapes with the fewest number of constraints. So some spaces are multi-purpose and some, like the atelier, are not. The views from the space and into it are also important. Small children can look out of the space they are in and see other spaces and things and people. It is a simple, basic but social landscape. In the nido *Iotti*, for example, there is a room overlooking the car park and the teachers are aware of the fact that each day the babies, who are just becoming mobile, crawl over to the window to re-enact their goodbyes to their parents. In this way the windows act as what might be called *security niches*. They are safe places to replay the emotional partings, over and over again.

Any space reflects the culture of those who make it. A nido consists of many cultural layers, the first of which is the beauty of the space itself. As you have already learned, this is evident in the simplicity of the design, the use of light and subtle colours, the well-tended plants, the furnishings sometimes designed and made by the parents and the attention to detail. In one nido there is a piece of furniture made by one of the parents. It has small doors, at the height of a toddler, each with a different type of open or closing device. There are keys in keyholes, handles, buttons to press, bolts to slide. The second cultural layer refers to the culture of the city and the region, and this is reflected in the organisation of space, which mirrors cooperation and cooperatives, people working and planning together. The piazza, evident in all the provision, is a very clear example of this. To have one in a Birmingham crèche, for example, would not make any sense, but in Reggio the piazza is an essential part of the city itself. Regional touches are apparent in some of the tools and materials used, the food the children eat and the languages spoken and heard. The documentation, so prominent in all the provision, pays tribute to the city of Reggio and its surroundings, as it displays paintings, drawings, photographs and other work associated with the many outings into the city and its surroundings. Reggio Children has produced a pack of postcards of drawings made by the children about their city. It is called *Reggio Tutta: the City as Seen by the Children*. Here are some of the things the children said about their city:

> At night the sky talks to the trees.
> In the city it smells wet.
> In Reggio everybody has a bike.
> The centre is like the centre of the world, where everything goes around it.

Then there is the very particular culture of each individual nido, which has been creating narratives, documenting them and storing them over years. They are the stories of the children and their families, their successes, their questions, their answers and their theories. They now cover three generations of children. Thus there are individual and group stories, particular ways of working and planning and a complex interweaving of the lives of the infants and toddlers with their teachers, families and communities. Then there is the vital aspect of home–nido links, which are prominent, essential and visible through many things. For example, the things the children bring to the nido to comfort them or play with or show to others and the things they take back from the nido. In most of the nidi there are collections of things the children have brought or gathered, and these are sometimes displayed in transparent plastic boxes. In addition, plastic bags travel to and fro between home and nido when children want or need to take something home or bring something into school.

As the children play, act, explore and express, they create their own culture. The environment supports all this and all the new relationships that form and bring new ideas. The common elements of all the provision are the creative solutions found, the care of the environment, the attention to detail and the reflection of the lived lives brought in by children and families.

A bill of three rights

In 1993 Malaguzzi laid out his thoughts on the rights of parents to have a real say in the education of their children, in what is sometimes referred to as a 'bill of three rights'. Developing equal and respectful partnerships with them was essential, and such partnership meant not only keeping parents informed about how well their children were doing, but asking for and listening to their views on all aspects of the lives of the children in the nidi:

> Parents have the right to participate freely and actively in the elaboration of the founding principles and in their children's experiences of growth, care and learning while entrusted to the public institutions ... there should be a presence and a role for parents such as the one valued by our institutions long tradition and experience.
>
> (Malaguzzi 1993: 9)

You may remember that in first chapter of this book we talked about how Malaguzzi shared some ideas with Bronfenbrenner, who saw the child as being situated within layers of culture, context and influence, going from the intimacy of the home to the surrounding neighbourhood and community and finally up to the very remote but often troubling influences of government policy.

Hall *et al.* examined the particular features of the both the nidi and the scuole dell'infanzia, which highlight the vital importance of partnerships with parents and families. We have talked about some of these, like the sensitive moment of parting from a parent each day, but we will examine them again. The first is the moment of arriving at the nido, making the transition from the extreme intimacy of the home to the less intimate environment of the nido. The Italian word *l'inserimento*, meaning this first transition from 'a focused attachment to parents and home to shared attachment that includes the adults and environment of the nido' (Malaguzzi 1998: 62) is used. The emphasis here is on the formation of new attachments and relationships, as well as on making the transition as easy as possible. It is accepted in Reggio that this process may take a long time and the phasing in is done slowly and carefully, a step at a time, on an individual basis, and working closely with the parents and their feelings and work requirements. As in many places in the UK work on this even begins before the child starts, including home visits. If you are interested in the details of how this is done you can find it explained in detail in Hall (2010). What is established as a result of this careful and slow process is a relationship of mutual trust, respect and understanding. The fact that many parents stay involved with the nido long after their toddlers have moved on is testament to this.

Another Italian word that does not translate easily is *partecipazione*. Literally translated it means participation, but in essence it means much more. Partecipazione is enshrined in Italian law and means the sharing and co-responsibility of families in both the construction and the management of the nido. In this way the operation of the nido is co-constructed by teachers and parents through discussion and debate, explanation and questioning. It is difficult to find anything that replicates this in the UK, despite valiant efforts on the part of some nurseries. The difference is the legal status of this requirement; this is something that came about through Malaguzzi's prolonged and strenuous argument and campaigns. Parents are invited to contribute to the discussion and the decisions made about how children learn and should be supported or taught. For Malaguzzi and those who followed on, this is an essential tool for social change. Rinaldi (2007) talks of schools being participatory places, where a dialogue with parents and participation by the town have always been part of the programme. As you can imagine, this is no easy way of working since it may be challenging to teachers or to parents, but at its heart is the determination to work for the best possible care and education for the always-competent child.

What is involved in much of the discussion is reflection on why things should be kept the same or changed, illustrated by examples of what children have said or done that shows their extraordinary abilities, even when the discussion focuses on babies and toddlers. Discussion and debate follows on from the detailed documentation that teachers engage in. What children say and do is recorded, made available for family members to see, analysed, considered and shared. The term used to describe this kind of recording of what children achieve is *pedagogical documentation*. It is very different from ticking a target on a test sheet or writing a comment. It involves active listening. This means that the teacher engaged in pedagogical documentation is genuinely interested in what it is that the child is trying to do, what question she has raised in her mind, what theory she has formed. By listening to what the child says to herself or others, intuiting what she is paying attention to or what has grabbed her interest, the teacher is able to come up with a theory of her own – this time about what is happening. Here is a small example to illustrate this, taken from Vecchi:

> Mattia is 10 months old. He crawls towards a cupboard and by sitting upright he can reach a ring-shaped handle on the drawer. At the same time he notices a metal teaspoon on the floor. He begins to pass the spoon through the door handle over and over again. The teachers do not know whether something in his experience has suggested that the spoon might pass though the handle and it is not easy for him to do. Each time he does it it drops on the floor and in doing that produces a sound which clearly pleases him because he does it again and again.

This is Vecchi's analysis of how adults might see this example of learning in action or active listening:

> At this point there might already be an initial difference in what people mean by a teacher's work. One person might observe the scene appreciatively, but let their interest end there because they do not see it as relevant to the work of an educator. Another teacher might carefully observe this small event, annotating all Mattia's explorations, because they are considered useful material to reuse with other children after suitable reflection. The teacher who has documented Mattia's game can thus begin a project offering a small context to children of the same age, situating it in an environment where other children can reproduce the significant phases in Mattia's explorations, highlighting and varying certain aspects of the perceptions such as size (both the hole through which the object is passed and the object itself), the degree of difficulty in passing the object through the hole, the height from which it falls, the materials it is made from, the surface it falls onto in order to introduce different, varying sound effects …

(Vecchi 2010: 39–40)

This seems a perfect explanation of just how important this type of active listening is to the whole of the pedagogy of Reggio. I chose this example because it is much more difficult to see what might be interesting in a child passing a spoon through a handle than to exclaim with wonder at the wonderful artwork produced. The processes are the same. The child is interested in something and begins to explore and express her developing ideas, thoughts and feelings. This expression might be in repeating a physical action over and over again to enjoy or understand what is happening; it may be in moving around a space in order to see how big it is, how many steps it takes to go from one spot to another; it may be in manipulating a lump of clay to try and see what shapes can be made and what these resemble and can be turned into. The child is using her hundred languages. The teacher, actively listening, records and documents what has been heard and seen, and then takes time to analyse it in order to understand it, learn from it and apply it to other situations or children.

Later in the book Vecchi gives a wonderful account of the partnership she had with the parents of Mattia, who themselves came to her with this delightful account of his learning at home.

> Mattia has just turned 11 months and for some time has known how to get down from the sofa and bed; he turns round on his bottom and slides down backwards onto the floor. This particular day, after getting down he wants to get back up on the bed again but the side is too high and despite his repeated efforts he cannot manage. He moves away and his parents think he has abandoned the idea but soon he comes back pushing a small plastic stool across the floor, which he places next to the bed and uses as a step to finally get up on to the bed.
>
> (Vecchi 2010: 130)

Not only does Vecchi record and keep this, she goes on to analyse it and apply it to what Mattia does over the following months. She tells us that now he uses many different household objects to stand on in order to reach switches and turn on the lights, which he loves doing. She then thinks about what it was in that first experience of making himself taller that enabled him to keep doing it and applying it to different situations. She suggests many factors – motivation, emotion, physicality, accompanying sounds, independence, effort required, success in attaining a goal. This is listening, watching, analysing, recording and documenting, working in genuine and equal partnership with parents and being respectful of the child's abilities.

The third Italian term not easy to translate is *gestione sociale*, which can loosely be translated to mean social management, which, in Reggio, is expressed as participation in the everyday experience and the formal management structures that support their preschools. I hope you remember the history of how these centres came about and how they arose from the ruins of two wars, the stranglehold of the church, the fight by women and workers to assert their rights and those of their children. Out of that came the formation of group of people from different backgrounds, all working to change the world, to make sure the children were never again be voiceless. In 1970 a national law put in place that the nidi should be under community management, with national government providing the funding; regional government taking charge of overall planning and the municipality responsible for community-based management. So the municipality – in this case Reggio Emilia – provided the pedagogical direction and supervision.

The third partner in the learning process

The environment in any nido or scuola dell'infanzia is seen as a partner in the learning process. Issues around time and space are very important and there has been an ongoing research project between the *Domus Academy of Milan* and Reggio Children, which resulted in a book called *Children, Spaces, Relations: Metaproject for an Environment for Young Children* (Ceppi and Zini 1998). Growing out of Malaguzzi's ideas about the importance of the environment, new preschools were designed with some concepts in mind. One of the key questions asked was what is it that school environments can teach children? In some places they teach children to be quiet, to differentiate between work and play, to answer and not ask questions, to make sure they do not make a mess, to sing only when it is time to sing; essentially to do as the adults tell them. You may have attended a school like that or even worked in one. The preschools in Reggio are very different. They are designed to reflect the values expressed by John Dewey, Vygotsky and Malaguzzi, who saw young children as being resourceful, questioning, competent, imaginative, creative and communicative beings. The best environment to support such beings is one that is rich and complex and that allows for children to set their own questions, follow their passions, try out their developing theories, talk and listen, share and participate, lead and follow. The underpinning thesis is that all children have a right to environments that will promote and support their hundred and more languages.

Taking it for granted that the environment is the third educator (the other two being the teachers assigned to each group of children), let us look at some of the features to be found in a nido or scuola dell'infanzia. All centres are made up of spaces large and small, thresholds, outdoor environments and places to meet, eat, play, share, sleep, be alone or with a friend or in a group or all together.

There is an *entrance*, which, as we have said, is a welcoming place for children and their families – a place that encourages communication. It also welcomes visitors by having on display a floor plan and the organisational structure of the centre. There is information about the teachers, about meetings or activities for parents, information about the city and more. As you now know, the move from being at home to being at a nido (l'inserimento) is seen as an essential part of becoming a member of the community of the nido. Throughout the entrance and beyond are low windows, with soft furnishings close by to encourage toddlers to spend time there to watch the birds or greet their friends. There are many low windows giving views of what is happening throughout the nido and also a small curtained space where children can play routines like 'Peekaboo', which Bruner defined as one of the essential rituals in language acquisition. This is a place for becoming part of the nido, looking and listening, using the languages of greeting and separation, of welcoming friends, watching what is going on, building trust and getting to know people new to the nido.

There is then the *piazza*, which replicates in function and spirit the town square – a place for meeting people, exchanging ideas, running about, drinking coffee, being social and sociable. This is the most public space in the building and has changing displays of what the children have been doing and saying, large mirrors, performance areas and a dressing up capsule (or small space). This is where children can meet one another, adults can meet one another, adults can meet children.

In the centre of the building is an open patio area sometimes called *a room without a ceiling*. This symbolises the connections between indoors and out. In the winter it is the internal garden and in summer a place to which children have free access.

Then there is the atelier, which is a workshop where children use expressive languages to develop their ideas. The word can be translated as 'studio', but it is more accurate to refer to it as a studio that is also a laboratory. The atelier may contain some specialised equipment and resources, but is essentially very much part of the nido physically, also promoting enquiry, investigation and expression and encouraging the use of spoken and other languages. For Malaguzzi, the presence of the atelier was at the heart of all he wanted to see:

> For us, the atelier had to become part of a complex design and, at the same time, an added space for searching, or better, for digging with one's own hands and one's own mind, and for refining one's own eyes, through the practice of the visual arts. It had to be a place for sensitising one's own taste and aesthetic sense, a place for the individual exploration of projects connected with experiences planned in the different classrooms of the school. The atelier had to be a place for researching motivations and theories of children from scribbles on up, a place for exploring variations in tools, techniques and materials with which to work. It had to be a place favouring children's logical and creative itineraries, a place for being familiar with similarities and differences of verbal and nonverbal languages.
>
> (Gandini 2005: 7)

It is an extraordinary vision that so clearly expresses his view of children, from the very youngest, being able to research, explore, express, use verbal and non-verbal languages, develop and refine their skills as they work alongside one another and often with someone – such as the atelierista, who is a trained artist. The purpose of the atelier is to provide a dedicated space where children will encounter beautiful, interesting and challenging things to excite their imagination and all the tools and resources they could need to develop their responses and communicate these in different ways. But just as importantly, it is also there to help the adults understand the very processes children use as they learn. With support and real attention, children come to be able to make their own decisions and choices about what to represent and in what way. In Vecchi's words, it helps children achieve cognitive and symbolic freedom as they use their languages to communicate.

Classrooms come off the central piazza and have direct access to the 'room with no ceiling'. They are flexible spaces, well equipped with low platform areas where groups can meet, light tables and pull-down screens. Each has a mini atelier, where children can engage in creative activities whenever they choose to. In some of the nidi there is a third small space, which is the quiet zone with low light levels. Even the youngest children can play with clay, build and construct, play and experiment with light and dark. Stories about and for the children are displayed at their eye level and are easy for them to examine.

The *dining room* and *kitchen* are seen as much part of learning as the rest of the place. Food plays an important role in the lives of the people of Reggio and the proximity of the kitchen to the other areas means that children can choose to go into the kitchens, to interact with the staff, draw what they see, ask the staff to make a cake for someone's birthday and more. The dining room consists of specially designed tables and chairs of the right size for small bodies. It is a room used for nothing else and where the social interaction at mealtimes is much valued.

In the *bathrooms* you will find mirrors everywhere, together with scents, music and textures so that the young child's use of her senses in learning is recognised and promoted.

Storage is designed to stimulate and enrich children's curiosity, creativity and communication. In the atelier there are open shelves for storage, allowing the children to make their own choices of what to use. The strong role of the arts in Italian culture is evident in all the preschools, as where you find manmade and natural materials in transparent containers or set on or in front of mirrors to allow for multiple views to capture the children's attention. Aspects of home are included – real flowers in vases, attractive plates to eat off, patterned table cloths and decorated plates. Breast-feeding mothers are welcomed in to feed their babies when they can.

The story of the Maramotti nido and how it came about

Giulia Maramotti was a famous figure in the world of designing and making women's clothes. In 2004 the *Maramotti Foundation*, set up in her memory, announced a competition for the designing and building of a new nido to be named after her. The competition was open to architects and engineers under the age of 35. This was to encourage young professionals from the region to design an educational space for the youngest children, inspired by the high quality of existing provision. The whole project was followed and documented by *Paola Cavazzoni*, who is a pedagogista. She said that the two young people who won the competition had done so because in their designs it was evident that they paid great attention to the potential experiences young children would enjoy and benefit from. So they designed a space open to the outdoors that had movable ateliers that could be placed closer to the building to be protected in the winter and further away during the summer. In their submission they talked about the importance of mobility (how easily young children could move around the spaces), transparency (how easy was it for them so see and be seen anywhere in the nido) and transformation (how the spaces could be changed).

One of the young artists, *Carlo Margini*, talked of how one of the ideas they kept in mind was the idea of continuous change. They were eager to create a space that was movable because they felt that daily changes might be worth considering, although they respected the need for the children to have a space that is familiar and stable.

The young teachers, new to the school like the children, noticed that the children were very interested in the building itself. They had watched it being built and looked at the photographs and drawings of work in progress. In some of these, taken from a distance, the building looks very like a toy construction. So the teachers bought construction equipment and asked parents to bring in anything they had to add to this collection. The teachers noticed that the children were beginning to be able to use the language of the construction materials they had access to. Margini commented that the very structure of the building was like a toy, from the point of view of the children.

Here we have a nido named after a fashion designer. Close by is the nido Choreia, named for the Greek word meaning a 'sung dance or a choir singing in unison'; another is the nido *Otello Sarzi*, named for a local puppet-maker and animator. You will be pleased to know that other preschools are named after people from the arts (for example *Vinci, Michelangelo, Neruda, Pascoli, Dante Aligheri, Anderson*); politics in the broadest sense (*Pablo Neruda, Salvador Allende, Ann Frank, Paolo Freire*); things in nature (sun and rainbow) and fiction (*Gulliver, Robinson, Peter Pan*). This is a city respecting not only its indigenous culture, but also the wider cultures from Europe and beyond.

Looking back, looking ahead

In this chapter we have looked particularly, but not exclusively, at the principles and values underpinning the development of the asili nidi for babies and toddlers. These came later than the scuole dell'infanzia but grew out of the fight by women in the region to ensure that their babies and toddlers had as much right to high-quality provision as their older siblings and friends. But by the time these came into existence, the commune had learned a great deal from monitoring the developments in the scuole dell'infanzia and, as a consequence, were able to adopt much of their philosophy into the design, staffing, organisation and principles of the nidi. Most particularly they were able to consider babies and toddlers as inherently curious and questioning, communicating and intuiting feelings and motives in others. In the next chapter we turn our attention to seeing early childhood education as political, in the sense of enabling young children to become equal citizens in their communities. To do this we extend Malaguzzi's reach by looking at some of the developments in other parts of Italy where, as in Reggio, early childhood provision is the site of democratic practice.

Chapter 9

Democracy and participation in early childhood education

> Education either functions as an instrument which is used to facilitate integration of the younger generation into the logic of the present system and bring about conformity or it becomes the practice of freedom, the means by which men and women deal critically and creatively with reality and discover how to participate in the transformation of their world.
>
> (Richard Shaull in his foreword to the first edition of Paulo Freire's *Pedagogy of the Oppressed*)

It is unlikely that the Brazilian philosopher, educationalist, radical thinker and teacher, *Paolo Freire*, ever met Loris Malaguzzi, but it is clear that they had many things in common, most significantly what the purpose of education should be. Both saw that generations of poor children had been educated through methods where power and knowledge rested with the teacher, with the students being seen as waiting to be 'educated'. There was an accepted body of knowledge that the children needed to acquire. Their interests and concerns were not to be taken into account. Children were expected to learn things by rote, answer questions put to them, not interrupt the teacher, be quiet and biddable and do as they were told. Both Freire and Malaguzzi saw this, in part, as explaining why generations of the children of the poor and the oppressed grew up to remain poor and oppressed. If your concerns, needs, ideas and interests are never addressed, how can you criticise the world in which you live? Education functioned as a method for integrating the young into the logic of the existing systems, status quo, power structures and class divides. Freire and Malaguzzi spent their working lives as committed educators working for the emancipation of these learners from this oppression. Freire's field was the education of adults – denied opportunities to learn to read and write, question and comment, judge and decide. His work was seen as so threatening in his native Brazil that he became an exile and spent his life developing his ideas of a *dialogic approach* to learning. Here learning takes place through dialogue between equals, where learners can ask questions, express ideas, make choices and develop critical and analytical skills. It is opposed to the traditional approach of what is often called the *banking model of education*: the teacher has the knowledge and transmits it to the empty vessel of the learner. Malaguzzi's focus, as you know, was on the youngest children, who were equally encouraged to question in order to become able to express their developing ideas, thoughts, concepts, hypotheses, critiques and evaluations. In short, both men worked to change society.

Nurseries as spaces for ethical and political practice (Thanks to Dahlberg and Moss, 2005: 1–2)

In developing an educational system some underpinning philosophy and set of values is always necessary. We have said something about the values on which Malaguzzi and Freire based their proposed educational programmes and systems. Here are some statements from booklets produced by some preschool settings in the UK and elsewhere. Read though them and think about what sort of vision of the purpose of early education you think dominates them. Do you, for example, think that the dominating purpose seems to be measuring the academic progress of the children, the management of their behaviour, the value for money or a consideration of the citizens the children will become? Or perhaps something quite different?

> *Rainbow Nursery* is over-subscribed largely because the children all achieve excellent results in their end of stage tests. Our results are published so that parents are able to make informed choices. Most children move easily from Rainbow Nursery to our two linked schools where they continue to do very well.

> Our reception class at *Blue Fields Primary School* is set up to be a space where children can use all means available to express their developing ideas, thoughts, concepts and feelings. The focus in the nursery has been on children learning through play and following their own interests. We try and maintain this in the reception class. In this richly diverse community we encourage children to use their first or home languages whilst they develop their fluency in English; parents are often in the room helping out in many ways and we take the children on outings into the local community and wider afield.

> The focus in *Cameron Nursery School* is on value for money. We are aware of the choices parents can make about where to let their youngest children begin their educational careers. We ensure that the time the children spend here is profitable, with some time each day devoted to learning the skills essential for reading, writing and mathematics. There is a strong daily focus on the learning of phonics. All children are put in

ability groups. They are tested regularly and parents are kept informed of their academic progress. We were recently assessed as an excellent centre.

The Madiba Centre is a place of safety for many of our children, who may experience difficult home lives owing to poverty, exclusion, discrimination or other factors. We aim to create an environment where each child and her or his family is respected. We make strong links with the families of the children and invite family members to get involved when they can. Although we are not richly resourced we are skilled and experienced at finding ways of using materials in the natural and made worlds which the children use to express their own thoughts and ideas.

What did you decide for each of these? You may have felt that some were easy to label and others less so, but hopefully you will have been able to see the differences – small as they may be – between them.

Dahlberg and Moss (2005) argue that our society, like America, is dominated by particular values, such as individual choice, competitiveness, certainty and universality. These values seem increasingly to apply to the wider developed world. Many countries are adopting the very language of these values – terms like success and failure, best and worst, market place, choice and value for money. This can be seen as the globalisation of not only the English language but of an Anglo-American discourse. There is also the prevailing notion that there can be no other way of being. It is taken for granted that all parents want the best for their children, but not necessarily for the children of others. For them, the best might mean academic success, which they are told and believe comes about through early and rigorous teaching rather than early and wide experience and learning. They are told and believe that their child will do best when she is with other children like her, because diversity, it is said, runs the risk of 'dumbing' down. Less privileged children might need different approaches or more support, which takes something away from their child. Individuality is to be celebrated. There is little sense of the child as set in the context of a community. This is essentially an anti-state, anti-welfare, neo-liberalist stance and it is for you to decide if it is what we should be promoting or challenging.

Working towards democratic practice

Malaguzzi, as you know, was a passionate believer in the scuole dell'infanzia and the asili nidi as spaces where democratic practice should and does take place. His whole educational philosophy was based on his determination that the children being educated should emerge as independent thinking, questioning, concerned, communicative members of their communities. He began, and remained attached to, a socio-historical and cultural view of education.

We know that he was an effective advocate for this philosophy and managed to persuade the commune and successive mayors and administrations to support his ideals philosophically and financially. The result is the famous preschool provision in Reggio Emilia. His message spread – initially to other towns in Emilia Romagna, and then further afield in Italy.

For example, further south in Tuscany, we find another system of preschool provision, less well known, less widespread, but based on similar ideals, appropriately developed or adapted to meet the particular history and context of each city or town. In the small city of Pistoia there are not only asili nidi for the youngest children and scuole dell'infanzia for the 3 to 6 year olds, but a wide range of additional facilities for children and their families. Like Reggio, Pistoia has put in place and developed a strong concept of the responsibility of public administration to create ways and means to enhance family participation in educational services. It has pioneered a system of diverse services and resources to reach out across the generations and communities of the city to discuss the needs of children and how to meet them, and how to build all of this into a positive view of childhood. Like Reggio, and influenced by Malaguzzi's thoughts, Pistoia made each setting a potential site for the development of questioning, thinking, rational and expressive future citizens.

Their system includes traditional child care centres, parent/child preschool programs, after-school enrichment classes and *AreaBambini*, with workshops that specialise in such areas as storytelling and oral tradition, nature and environment, computers and technology, and the visual and manual arts (*Galardini, Giovannini and Iozelli* 1999).

Pistoia, close to Florence, is an agricultural and industrial centre and a provincial capital. Its main industries included the construction of city buses and subway cars from 1960 to 1994 that were exported to the United States. More recently the city's wealth has been fostered by growing plants and flowers to be exported all over Europe, and the manufacture of leather and metal goods, glass, textiles, and footwear. It is close to Prato, a city famed for the cloth made locally and the garment industry, which, sadly, is now in recession as the Chinese influence grows. The city rose to prominence in the twelfth and thirteenth centuries, and its citizens made important contributions to architecture and sculpture. It has much in common with Reggio Emilia, but also much that is unique. One of the great things about preschool provision in many of the regions of Italy is its responsiveness to local needs, history, people and more.

Some illustrative case studies

We will start by looking at one of the scuole dell'infanzia in Pistoia, looking for evidence that it is a site for democratic practice. *La Filastrocca* opened in 1970, originally under the name of *Fornaci*, which means 'furnace' or 'kiln', the name of the neighbourhood in which it was located, where there was a large factory that produced and fired bricks. This is a section of the city that contains many new residents, some from other areas of the country, some immigrants, many relatively disadvantaged and poor, having come to the town to seek work. Some speak languages other than Italian; some need special support with respect to acquiring and passing on to their children the skills leading to educational and economic advancement.

Fornaci was totally renovated and enlarged in 1990 and renamed La Filastrocca, which means 'nursery rhymes'. You may remember that many of the nursery schools in Reggio Emilia are named after philosophers, thinkers, artists or famous people in the worlds of the arts or the political world of those seeking to improve lives. The names of schools and settings are clearly significant. At Fornaci, the teachers invited all the children who had previously attended the school to send in their suggestions of names for the newly redesigned scuola. La Filastrocca emerged as the favourite and an image of *Mago*, the magician, was chosen as the symbol of the school.

La Filastrocca adopts a philosophy rooted in community values, respect for the past and looking to a better future. Families are essential to their enterprise and the staff seek to draw on the contributions of all the adults involved – teachers, parents and community members to create and work towards a shared direction to make the school a true learning community. It is a community that gives importance to rediscovering traditions and valuing the stories of the grandparents. *Lella Gandini*, writing about the provision in Pistoia, noted that this region of Tuscany is famous for its storytelling tradition (it is close to where *Carlo Collodi* wrote the children's classic *Pinocchio*) and there remains a commitment to children's literature and fairy tales. In the early years of this scuola teachers began to tell stories in order to revive the ancient tradition of storytelling, and later extended this to include making and sharing narrative, negotiation, role play and more. La Filastrocca began to deliver a culture of oral storytelling, acting, story making and narration, negotiation, reading and writing. In doing this they drew on and showed respect for the skills, experience and knowledge of others.

You will remember that the provision in Reggio Emilia depends largely on the ateliers. Something very similar, but developed locally, is the system of laboratories that are to be found in all the scuole and some of the alternative provision discussed below. La Filastrocca, for example, has its own reading laboratory that has been active the past 20 years. It is called *Paging Through the Rainbow* and involves all the children and their families in literacy and book borrowing. Like the ateliers in Reggio, the laboratori are situated within the schools and are well resourced, each with a particular focus. Examples of the areas of focus include promoting pretend play and the world of make-believe, things for games, playing to explore and playing to make a theatre, another way of looking and speaking and writing.

AreaBambini are spaces in the city for babies and children (aged between 3 and 12 years), available in the mornings or afternoons where they can meet other babies and children in an environment designed to allow them to explore games and space. Parents meet one another here and often there is a qualified adult on hand to help address pedagogical or other issues. The spaces are both indoors and outside in gardens. There are four of these – yellow, blue, green and red – and within each are laboratories. In the yellow *AreaBambini* the laboratory is called *Di Bocca in Bocca* (which means 'from mouth to mouth') and is dedicated to storytelling and role play: in essence on narrative. In the green *AreaBambini* children are invited to explore the natural world and can become involved in growing things, looking after animals and using the products of the earth. In the red *AreaBambini* the focus is more on graphic representations and looking at ways of making images old and new.

There are also small spaces (*Spazio Piccolissimi*) for babies between 0 and 18 months, accompanied by a parent or carer, where the adults can meet and exchange thoughts and ideas as they watch their babies in these specially dedicated spaces. They are open on weekday mornings and places need to be reserved. For babies from 18 months to 3 years who do not attend a nido, there are *Le Case Degli Orsi* ('houses of the bears'), which they can attend two days a week either in the mornings or afternoons.

In addition there is a specialist library for babies and children based on an understanding that books can be actors in dialogues between children and others – friends and peers, older children, parents, grandparents and other adults. It is through these interactions that children can encounter, explore and even create possible worlds.

Looking north

Reggio Emilia, as you know, has no curriculum. The Norwegian curriculum for early years education is 34 pages long, compared to that for our country, which most recently stands at 128 pages. Ours is prescriptive and linked to many early learning goals. It is full of directives for teachers, pointing out developmental milestones to be attended to. It can be seen is a guide for technicians rather than a principled document designed to be interpreted by trained and respected professionals. Nowhere in our curriculum do the words democracy appear, yet in the Norwegian curriculum there is mention of the role of kindergartens being to lay the foundations for active participation in democratic society. This has echoes in the Swedish curriculum, which states that democracy forms the foundation of the preschool and that all activity should be carried out in accordance with the associated democratic values. The Icelandic curriculum for preschools says that one of the principle objectives of all preschool education is to enable children to become independent, reflective, active and responsible citizens, able to live and thrive in a democratic society.

Peter Moss, in his seminal paper *Bringing Politics into the Nursery* (2007), tells of a visit he made to an Italian city with a rich experience in early childhood, where the head of services described the project – a 30-year long project – as a 'local cultural project of childhood'. This phrase is one that needs unpicking to be fully understood. Drawing on Moss, I take it to mean what happens when there is the political commitment together with the willingness of those in the community to get involved in genuinely collective decision-making in order to take responsibility for all children of the community and their education, in its widest sense. This means having to think not only about what provision there is, but also about what takes place within the provision. In order to do this successfully, those making the decisions (parents, teachers, trades unionists, workers, community members, local authority members and more) all need to really know what takes place within the provision so that they are able to evaluate it with the help of one another and within the terms they have agreed.

One of the essential features of democratic practice is that of documentation, which we have discussed throughout this book. Hoyuelos (2004) reminds us that it was one of Malaguzzi's key principles and behind it is the idea of the transparent school. Where teachers and others closely document and share what happens there is a true act of democracy and it makes what happens within the school visible to all. A reminder that the documentation we are talking of is more than child observation – not intended to measure what a child can or cannot do. It is an essential research and pedagogical tool, designed to show what is being done and said by the children and those interacting with them.

Is this enough?

It is all very well for any preschool or setting to become democratic within its enclosing walls. Clearly any place that involves parents and people from the community and that ensures that the voices of children are not only heard but attended to will be doing something towards ensuring that those children grow up feeling part of their community. But the question of whether this is enough is important. We could say, borrowing from Bronfennbrenner, that this constitutes democracy at the micro-level, and if we want genuine and widespread societal changes we need to go beyond the micro.

We touched on this when we looked at the differences in ideology between the governments of the Nordic countries and the UK, but let us take a more detailed and nuanced look to analyse what happens at a local government level.

We have seen how in Reggio and later other regions of Italy, despite a central government showing little if any commitment to providing services for its young children and their families, municipalities became determined to support a range of expensive initiatives with the understanding that quality preschool provision was not only morally and ethically sound but also economically worthwhile. We do not have to look very far to find a central government, together with local government, considering this issue very carefully. As you read it do remember that it has been profoundly influenced by the work of Malaguzzi and his followers. It comes from the Early Years Framework drawn up by the Scottish Government in 2008. As you read it, look out for things that suggest to you a profound understanding of what a country needs to do to change its social structures through empowering everyone from their early lives to become full and active citizens in their communities. I have italicised some phrases that seem significant to me:

> This (framework) provides the basis for a new vision for early years that reflects the high ambitions that the Scottish Government and local government have for early years.
>
> The vision establishes *a new conceptualisation of early years* – that children should be valued and provided for within communities; the importance of strong, sensitive relationships with parents and carers; the right to a high quality of life and access to play; the need to put children at the centre of service delivery; to provide more support through universal services when children need it; and that children should be able to achieve positive outcomes irrespective of race, disability or social background.
>
> *Parents and communities play a crucial role* in outcomes for children. That role needs to be valued by parents and communities themselves, but also supported by the community planning process. The vision also highlights the importance of high quality, flexible and engaging services delivered by a valued and appropriately qualified workforce in delivering the ambitions of this framework.

Putting the vision into action

These ambitions cannot be achieved by a business-as-usual approach. Transformational change is required, and ten elements of transformational change have been identified. These include:

- A coherent approach.
- Helping children, families and communities to secure outcomes for themselves.
- Breaking cycles of poverty, inequality and poor outcomes in and through early years.
- A focus on engagement and empowerment of children, families and communities.

- Putting quality at the heart of service delivery.
- Services that meet the needs of children and families.
- Improving outcomes and children's quality of life through play.
- Simplifying and streamlining delivery.
- More effective collaboration.
- Using the strength of universal services to deliver prevention and early intervention.
    (http://www.scotland.gov.uk/Resource/Doc/257007/0076309.pdf)

It is a good start and certainly uses some of the ideas embedded in thinking about democratic practice. For me, however, it is still largely hide-bound by using some of the language of competition, individual achievement and the market.

Moss (2007) tells us that there are four key activities that citizens must engage in to ensure democratic practice.

1   Making decisions about the purposes and the practices and the environment of the school, nursery, crèche or setting.
2   Becoming enabled to evaluate the quality of the pedagogical work going on in these settings through participatory methods like documentation, being involved in discussions, invited into the settings, joining debates, offering opinions and being taken notice of and heard.
3   Contesting dominant discourses which means challenging accepted ideas or ways of doing things, the language of the market place and the use of measures of individual achievement such as testing, streaming and more.
4   And finally, enabling change to take place. In Reggio the education and care of young children was moved away from the control of the church, for example. In many UK settings practitioners are working hard to ensure that young children can continue to learn through following their own interests despite outside attempts to get them to abandon such open-ended approaches for more outcomes-focused behaviour.

Looking back, looking ahead

This has been a book looking at the ideas and the influence of Loris Malaguzzi. We have looked at the roots of his thinking, the effects on him of what was happening around him in his early life and his developing and evolving philosophy about children, childhood, pedagogy and power. We have seen how hard he worked to ensure that local politicians in his area came to understand what he was trying to do and then supported him and continued to support him throughout his life and beyond. We have examined how his ideas spread, sometimes successfully (as where other local governments understood the need to provide the highest quality of early childhood education and care, and found ways of funding it) and sometimes less so, where places around the world think it enough to call themselves schools based on a Reggio Emilia curriculum and encourage children to produce pretty pictures.

This book is designed to help you identify just what it is in Malaguzzi's approach that allowed the seemingly miraculous provision to develop and grow and expand, so that now there are many young children who are benefitting from being invited to ask their own questions, develop and change their own theories, share their thoughts and ideas and know that becoming critical is not only acceptable but desirable. And there are many adults who see their roles as teachers as being researchers, documenters and partners in a complex, intricate, interactive, dynamic and ever-changing series of learning events.

Last words

How better to end this book than with words from Malaguzzi himself? I found this online and think if makes a fitting thought to end with. For me, it summarises his respectful approach to teaching and learning:

> Teachers – like children and everyone else – feel the need to grow in their competences; they want to transform experiences into thoughts, thoughts into reflections, and reflections into new thoughts and new actions. They also feel a need to make predictions, to try things out, and to interpret them … Teachers must learn to interpret ongoing processes rather than wait to evaluate results.
>
> (Edwards *et al.* 2011: 48–9)

Glossary

A public place Malaguzzi talked of preschools as being public places, by which he meant that they were rooted in the community and the culture of the community.

A quality place Another of Malaguzzi's terms, this time reminding people that where a child goes for a large part of her life needs to be a place that is attractive, well kept, welcoming, sensitively designed to meet the needs of adults and where things from the cultures of the children are on display.

Active listening The listening where one person pays real attention to what is being said and done in order to clearly understand what the speaker is interested in, paying attention to, raising questions about, developing theories of or expressing.

Alienation This means not being included, made to feel different and sometimes inferior or othered in some way. It is something unpleasant to experience.

Amiable school A place where the children and the adults feel happy to spend their time.

Atelier A French word meaning 'studio', but used in Reggio Emilia to mean a workshop or laboratory; a place of discovery, experimentation, the use of different ways of representing and re-representing ideas and research. There is one in every preschool.

Atelierista The atelierista works in the preschools, based primarily in the atelier. Initially atelieristi all had some art qualification although that is no longer the case. They work with children, alongside teachers, and play a very important role in developing projects, helping children develop essential skills, giving them the technical vocabulary to support these skills. They are closely involved in both documentation and research and play an essential role in professional development.

Banality Means the ordinary, not very relevant or interesting. Similar to mundane.

Banking education Where the teacher holds the knowledge and the power, the learner is seen as an empty vessel or a blank state to be written on.

Bonding   The term used to describe a close relationship, particularly but not solely between mother and child.

Boundaries   It means the line between one thing and another, where the line may be only notional. So there may be a boundary between fact and fiction or a boundary between art and science.

Bourgeoisie   This word literally means the middle class.

Casa dei Bambini   Literally means the house of babies (or young children).

Children's theories   Children, even the very young ones, develop theories about the things and people and events in their worlds, and express these through their questions, their drawings, their conversations or any other means. It is important to listen attentively in order to find these theories and to take them seriously. As children interact and learn, they confirm, change or abandon these theories for more appropriate and mature ones.

Chronosystem   One of Bronfennbrenner's layers of context, this one relates to time.

Cognitive conflict   A clash of ideas, opinions, values or principles.

Combative   This word means to stand up for or fight for something, perhaps something you value or believe.

Communism   A political philosophy and system based on the notion that a fair society is one where people have equal rights, an equal voice and are in control of the means of production.

Context   This means where something happens but is broader than being just about a place. The context includes the people present, and the ideas, values and principles. It is closely bound to culture and is extremely important in the work of Malaguzzi and his colleagues.

Critique   One of the things that children become able to do in Reggio preschools is to be able to critique their own work and that of others. The ability to make a judgement is very important and certainly only rarely evident in provision for young children in the UK.

Cultural layers   Any child is born into a culture, initially the very close one of the home. Beyond that are other layers of culture. The idea is evident in the work of Bronfennbrenner.

Culture   A word with many meanings and many layers of meaning. In its simplest form it means the sum of all the socially passed-on behaviour patterns, artefacts, objects, beliefs, institutions and other products of human work and thought.

Cultural hegemony   Gramsci's ideas about how to change society through challenging the accepted ways of doing things.

Decentre   The ability to see things from the point of view of someone else. Piaget believed that young children could not do this, but it is evident that they can since we often see one young child comforting another who is distressed. Doing this implies that the child can put herself in the shoes of someone else.

Democracy   The system of governing whereby all people have a vote and the ways in which things operate is open and transparent.

Democratic   A system that seeks to ensure that everyone has an equal say. It does not, of course, always operate perfectly.

Democratic education   A system of education where students and staff participate equally in decision-making through systems like school councils. You may notice that the definition does automatically include other stakeholders like parents.

Dialogic education   This is the kind of education where children or other learners are not given knowledge, but are seen to be actively making sense, asking questions, developing theories and exchanging ideas. The opposite of this is the blank slate or empty vessel approach, often known as 'banking education'.

Documentation   For those in Reggio Emilia this is about much more than simply recording events, precisely because it is part of the whole educational enterprise where the teachers are gathering evidence that needs to be considered and analysed in order to affect learning and development.

Documenter   The person documenting the processes seen and heard. In Reggio teachers, *pedagogisti* and *atelieristi* are documenters.

Dyad   This is a pair or a twosome.

Exosystem   The wider environment in which the child is not personally engaged but which affects her in some way. This could be the workplace of the parent, as the child can be affected if the mother has to work unsocial hours, or the father loses his job, or just comes home in a bad mood.

Expressive language   These are the hundred languages of the children – the ways in which they can expressive their feelings. They might include drama, role play, dressing up, painting, drawing, dancing, making, singing and more.

Fascism   Extreme right wing groups that promote the superiority of one group of others. The extreme example was of the Nazis (National Socialists) in Germany and Mussolini's fascists in Italy. But it is still present in the rise of many extreme groups throughout Europe and beyond.

Fatigue and joy   Everyday words, but used to describe the extremes of emotion that can characterise powerful learning experiences.

Flexible   Another everyday word that means a system that is not rigid or pre-determined but allows for teachers, in this case, to follow the leads given by children.

Follower   The teacher, as follower, allows the child to develop an individual or a shared interest in something and follows the child in the sense of taking note of what is happening and responding to it through providing help, resources or suggestions.

Formative experience   An experience that plays a role in shaping the development of someone. For me, a formative experience was being in hospital as a small child with nothing to do except learn to read.

Forum   Traditionally in Roman society this was a meeting place and in many ways it is still is. Bruner used the term to describe how the exchange of thoughts and ideas allows those involved to make and change culture. He used the term with regard to education.

Gestione sociale   An Italian phrase meaning 'social management' and used in Reggio to explain the commitment to ensuring that all stakeholders have a voice in the management of the learning and development of the preschool children.

Hand control to the children   Just what it says. This is where teachers watch and listen and follow the lead given by children. it is more difficult than it sounds and means trusting the children enough to let them be in control.

Hegemony   Means the leadership or use of power by one group over others.

Homogeneous methods   These are methods that are largely the same as one another.

Hundred languages   Malaguzzi's way of describing the seemingly unlimited ways in which people can express their questions, thoughts, feelings and ideas. I apply the same term to describe the responses that teachers make when they pay attention to what children say and so.

Ideological   Believing in something; having an ideology.

Ideological struggle   Ideological struggle means deciding between competing thoughts or ideas, systems or practices.

Inclusive community   An inclusive community is one that ensures that everyone has an equal voice in it.

Initiator   The person who starts or initiates something.

Intent participation   This is the term used for where someone really attends to every detail of what is happening. It can be applied to newborn babies, children and adults.

Intention   A goal or aim in the broadest sense. Not really used to cover something like being able to check something off a tick list. The goal needs to have some ideological underpinning.

Interpersonal   It means just what it says – between people. So it refers to almost every encounter you can imagine between two or more people.

Interpersonal cognitive constructions   A very wordy way of describing what happens when individuals solve problems or reach conclusions through encountering some disagreement with others.

Interpreter   An everyday term to describe someone who makes sense of something.

Intrapersonal   'Intra' means 'within', so this term describes what happens within the individual mind or self.

Joint enterprise   Where two or more people work together on the same topic or project.

L'inserimento   Italian word to describe all that is put in place to welcome children and families to the provision. It means more than merely 'welcome'.

Laboratori   Italian word for 'workshop' or 'laboratory', used primarily in Pistoia and other Tuscan cities to refer to the research-based areas set aside in preschools.

Laissez-faire   A term used to describe economic ways of dealing, meaning a situation where it is everyone for herself, with few rules.

Large issues   A term used to indicate things like life and death, fears and concerns, issues that may be difficult to discuss or share.

Liveable   Malaguzzi wanted schools to be liveable places, by which he meant friendly, welcoming, inclusive and non-threatening.

Macrosystem   One of Bronfennbrenner's layers of culture, it is probably the outermost layer being made up of cultural values, customs and laws.

Marginalisation   Marginalisation is where an individual is left to feel as though she does not belong to the group and is kept at its margins.

Market stalls   A term used by Malaguzzi to refer to what we might called activities – things like a home corner, block play area and so on.

Means of production   Means of production is a Marxist term for work or labour.

Mesosystem   This is the second most intimate of Bronfennbrenner's layers of culture – just beyond the immediacy of the family and describing where the family intersects with other things like school, religion and neighbourhood.

Messing about   What children do when they seek meaning. We might call it play.

Microsystem   The most intimate of Bronfennbrenner's layers of culture, this is made of the family, school and neighbourhood.

Multi-symbolic   Where more than one kind of symbol is used. In the theatre, for example, you might find acting, dance, music, painting, making and more.

Municipality   The equivalent of our local authorities.

Narrative   The making of a story in order to make sense of it and share it with others.

Neoliberalist   A debased term, literally meaning 'new liberal' but used here to indicate a system that sets out to ensure that the rich and powerful remain rich as the poor remain poor.

Nido   Italian word meaning, literally, 'nest', but used to describe the centres of infants and toddlers.

Non-verbal languages   Things like gesture, facial expression, tone of voice and more.

Observer   A person who observes in the sense of listening, watching and thinking about what has been seen or done, recording it, sharing it and watching again.

Palette of languages   A metaphor for Malaguzzi's hundred languages.

Partecipazione   Italian word meaning 'participation', but in reality meaning much more than the sort of parental participation we are used to. Here it refers to a genuine, respectful and equal exchange of ideas, views and expertise. It is a two-way process, not top down.

Pedagogy   A word used widely in Europe but less so here it means the art and/or science of teaching.

Pedagogy of listening   One of the cornerstones of Malaguzzi's philosophy, this describes the work being done to ensure that all teaching and learning is based on the cycle of observation, recording, analysing, discussing, making a change and starting the cycle all over again.

Pedagogy of relationship   Another of Malaguzzi's cornerstones, this one referring to the absolute imperative of ensuring that all learning is based on the interactions between children and children, adults and adults, adults and children. More than that, it means ensuring that all teaching and learning is set in the context of seeing the child as being an individual set in a family, with a particular history, attachments, culture, language and relationships.

Phase of learning   A very specific term used to describe what happened in Reggio after the Second World War, when people were described as learning by doing.

Political   Used primarily to explain aspects of government.

Political practice   Ways of operating that allow everyone involved both to have a voice and use it. It depends on being prepared to be critical and to accept criticism.

Possessive pronoun   The word 'our', which suggests ownership or possession.

Potential   Capacity in the sense of what is possible.

Power relationships   Gramsci was interested in this and wrote about it, considering if it was influential on Malagzuzzi's thinking, since it illustrated much of what had taken place in many places prior to the end of the war. Power rested in the hands of the wealthy and the church and this meant that workers, peasants and poorer people had no power and no access to power.

Pragmatic   This means something very close to practical and emphasises the importance of learning by doing and not only by attending to theory or dogma.

Progettazione   This is the Italian word for 'project', but it is used to describe something far more complex and long term than what is called 'project-based education' here or in the USA. According to Annamaria Mucchi, the verb *progettare* means to design, to plan, to devise or to project (in the technical engineering sense). The noun *progettazione*, in the educational context and in Reggio Emilia, means the opposite of *programmazione*, which is used to talk of a predefined curriculum or programme or stages or learning and development. So progettazione is more global and flexible, and considers how the initial hypotheses made about all aspects of education are subject to change as the work progresses. I think this makes very clear how different this is from a project per se.

Protagonists   Those who play a part.

Raggio di Luce   Literally 'ray of light', this is the name given to the atelier situated in the International Centre. It has a science focus.

Represent   To express your ideas, thoughts, questions or theories in any way you choose.

Re-represent   Having represented your feelings, thoughts or ideas once, you may choose to represent them again or re-represent them. This enhances and consolidates your learning.

Reason and emotion   Sometimes regarded as two opposing approaches, they are regarded as essential and contributory aspects of learning.

Reciprocal respect   Regarded as an essential part of learning, it refers to how respectful adults and children are of each other's ideas and feelings.

Research   The process of gathering evidence in support of a theory or to create a new theory.

Resistance   As used in this book, the resistance refers to those who united against fascism and often had to wage guerrilla warfare and live underground.

Respect   Treating others as equals in all things, which means paying attention to what they say and do rather than either dismissing it or paying lip service to it.

Respectful reciprocity   This is the phrase for a really vital aspect of pedagogy in Reggio Emilia. It is where the children, the learners (alongside other children and/or adults), are sharing a focus of interest or attention and working together in order to achieve a goal or answer a question they have set.

Responsive   What teachers need to be. In Reggio the whole documentation cycle involves the adults in reflecting on what they have seen and heard and being responsive to this. This might mean offering the child resources or tools, scaffolding learning, reminding children of what has already happened, helping children take a new line or more.

Scaffolding   A term coined by Bruner and drawn from 'building', where a scaffold supports a building in construction. Here it refers to the ways in which more experienced learners can help children take the next step in learning. The aim is for the child to be able to do something that they can do with help, be able to do this without help. It is towards independence.

Scientific languages   These could include the language and processes of mathematics, chemistry, biology and physics – so in terms of young children might refer to counting, manipulation of numbers, measuring, comparing, considering living and non-living things, properties of light or water or clay and so on.

Scuola dell'infanzia   The equivalent of preschool, nursery school or nursery class.

Secular   Not determined by any religious beliefs.

Shared enterprise   Something being worked on my more than one person.

Social capital   The things that link people to one another within their communities.

Social representation   The idea that words become imbued with meanings particular to groups in society. Think of lawyer or doctor jargon and how difficult it is for us to access.

Socialism   A political and economic theory that advocates that the means of production should be held by the people, the workers. Its opposite is said to be capitalism, where it is clear that the power and wealth are held by the already powerful and relatively rich.

Societal hegemony   This refers to how power is held in any society and the contribution each individual makes to this.

Sociocultural   A way of looking at the world that takes account of both society and culture, which means that context is always important.

Socio-historical   A way of looking at the world which takes account of how things have been organised over periods of time.

Special rights   In Reggio this is the term used where we might use 'special needs'.

Stakeholder   Those involved in any enterprise.

The third partner   A term used in Reggio to refer to the role played by the environment in early childhood education.

Transgressing   Means not conforming, being prepared to challenge and question and sometimes to break the rules.

Transformation   Means changing one thing into another.

Transformative   Something that brings about change.

Transparency   Something that can be seen through.

Transparent school   A school or setting where the practice – all aspects of practice – is made apparent to all stakeholders.

Triad   A group of three.

Unpredictable   Something not expected.

Zone of proximal development   Vygotsky's notional gap between what a child could do unaided if supported by a more experienced learner in moving from what the she already demonstrates she can do either unaided or with help. It is scaffolding that allows the child to close the gap.

Bibliography

Note: This has been a difficult bibliography to compile for several reasons. Many of the references have involved very small pieces found online. This is due to the ongoing popularity of Reggio Emilia, which results in many small articles being published. Some are difficult to attribute accurately; some are conference papers or records given to me as personal notes; some of the books referred to have several editions and there may be some discrepancy in terms of page numbers, where I have a more recent edition than the one cited. I have done my best to ensure that everything is referenced but it is possible that there are omissions and errors, for which I apologise.

Abbott, L. and members of the BERA Early Years Special Interest Group, 'Early Years Research: Pedagogy, Curriculum and Adult Roles' in *Training and Professionalism*. 2003. http://www.niched.org/docs/bera_report%20.pdf

Achtner, Wolfgang, 'Obituary: Loris Malaguzzi' in *The Independent*. 1 April 1994.

Adorni, D. and Magagnoli, S., 'For the sake of development? Municipal government and local development in Emilia Romagna and Turin (1945–78)' in The Annals of the Stefan cel Mare University of Suceava, fascicle of the Faculty of Economics and Public Administration. 11:13. 2011. http://www.seap.usv.ro/annals/ojs/index.php/annals/article/viewFile/385/394

Barsotti, A., Dahlberg, G., Gothson, H. and Asen, Gunnar. 'Early Childhood Education in a Changing World – a practice-oriented research project'. Paper presented at third European conference on the quality of Early Childhood Education, Chalkidiki. September 1993.

Bruner, J., *Actual Minds, Possible Worlds*. Cambridge, MA: Harvard University Press 1986.

Bruner, J., *Making Stories: Law, Literature, Life*. Harvard Press 2004.

Brunton, P. and Thornton, L., *Understanding the Reggio Approach: Early Years Practice*. Abingdon and New York: Routledge 2005.

Cavallini, I., Filippini, R., Trancossi, L. and Vecchi, V. (series directors), *We write shapes that look like a book*. Reggio Children 2008.

Children in Europe 6: 'Celebrating 40 years of Reggio Emilia: the pedagogical thought and practice underlying world renowned early years services in Italy'. http://www.childreninscotland.org.uk/html/pub_tshow.php?ref=PUB0082

Dahlberg, G. and Moss , P., *Ethics and Politics in Early Childhood Education*. Abingdon and New York: Routledge 2005.

Dahlberg, G. in Penn, H. (ed.), *Early Childhood Services: Theory, Policy and Practice.* Buckingham, Philadelphia: Open University Press 2000.

Day, Carol Brunson, 'Pioneers in Our Field: Loris Malaguzzi – Founder of the Reggio Emilia Approach in Early Childhood Today'. May 2001. http://www.scholastic.com/teachers/article/pioneers-our-field-loris-malaguzzi-founder-reggio-emilia-approach (accessed 17 November 2011).

Drummond, M. J., 'Everything is Beginning' in *ReFocus* 1 2005: 4–5.

Drummond, Mary Jane, 'Learning partners' in *TES* newspaper. 2004. www.tes.co.uk/article.aspx?storycode=398895 (accessed 10 January 2012).

Dunne, J., 'Childhood and citizenship: A conversation across modernity' in *European Early Childhood Education Research Journal* 14:1. 2006: 5–19.

Edwards, C. P., 'Democratic Participation in a Community of Learners: Loris Malaguzzi's Philosophy of Education as Relationship' posted at DigitalCommons at University of Nebraska. 1995. http://digitalcommons.unl.edu/famconfacpub/15/

Edwards, C., Gandini, L. and Forman, G. (eds.), *The Hundred Languages of Children: The Reggio Emilia Experience in Transformation.* Santa Barbara, Denver and Oxford: Praeger 2011.

Egan. B. A., 'Learning conversations and listening pedagogy: the relationship in student teachers' developing professional identities' in *European Early Childhood Education Research Journal* 17:1. 2009: 43–56.

Eskeson, K., 'Remida Denmark' in *ReFocus* 2007: 4–9.

Fahlman, P., 'Reggio Emilia' at NAEYC 2000. http://www.nauticom.net/www/cokids/reggio.html

Freire, Ana Maria and Macedo, D. (eds.), *The Paulo Freire Reader.* New York and London: Continuum 2001.

French, G., 'Children's early learning and development: a research paper' commissioned by National Council for Curriculum and Assessment (NCAA). 2007. http://www.ncca.ie/en/curriculum_and_assessment/early_childhood_and_primary_education/early_childhood_education/how_aistear_was_developed/research_papers/early_learning_and_dev_summary.pdf

Galardini, Giovannini and Iozelli. 1999 (paper is under review so we are not allowed to reference it).

Gandini, L., 'Fundamentals of the Reggio Emilia approach to early childhood education' in *Young Children* 49:1. 1993: 4–8.

Gandini, L., *In the Spirit of the Studio: Learning from the Atelier of Reggio Emilia.* New York: Teachers College Press 2005.

Gandini, L., 'History, Ideas and Basic Principles: An Interview with Loris Malaguzzi in Edwards' in Gandini, L. and Forman, G. (eds.), *The Hundred Languages of Children: The Reggio Emilia Experience in Transformation.* Santa Barbara, Denver and Oxford: Praeger 2011.

Giamminuti, S., 'For Beauty, for culture, for memory, for storytelling: Building learning communities through pedagogical documentation' in *Educating Young Children: Learning and Teaching in the Early Childhood Years.* http://www.ecta.org.au/_dbase_upl/Article%20_SGiamminuti.pdf

Giaretta, M., 'The research approach of PLAY-SOFT: Furnishings for flexible and responsive environments'. Studio UK.

Giudici, C., 'When pedagogy and atelier meet' interview reported in Vecchi, V., Giudici, C., Grasselli, G. and Morrow, L., *Children, Art, Artists: the Expressive Languages of Children, the Artistic Language of Alberto Burri*. Reggio Emilia: Reggio Children 2004: 144–53.

Hall, Ellen, 'What Professional Development in Early Childhood Science Will Meet the Requirements of Practicing Teachers?' SEED Papers from the STEM Early Education and Development Conference. 2010. http://ecrp.uiuc.edu/beyond/seed/hall.html

Hall, K., Hogan, M., Ridgway, A., Murphy, R., Cunneen, M. and Cunningham, D., *Loris Malaguzzi and the Reggio Emilia Experience* in *Library of Educational Thought* 23. London and New York: Continuum 2010.

Hawkins, D., 'Malaguzzi's Story, Other Stories and Respect for Children' in Edwards, C., Gandini, L. and Forman, G. (eds.), *The Hundred Languages of Children: The Reggio Emilia Experience in Transformation*. Santa Barbara, Denver and Oxford: Praeger 2011.

Hoyuelos, A., *Le etica en el pensamiento y obra pedagogica de Loris Malaguzzi*. Barcelona: Octaedro 2004.

Jones, L., 'Resource Roundup' in *Teaching Artist Journal* 4:2. 2009: 136–44.

Jones, D. D., Elders, L. and Fawcett, M., 'Reflecting on the Reflective Cycle' in *ReFocus* 9. 2009: 12–13.

Katz, L. and Cesarone, B., *Reflections on the Reggio Emilia Approach*. ERIC/Junior 1994.

Krechevsky, M. and Stork, J., 'Challenging Educational Assumptions: Lessons from an Italian-American collaboration' in *Cambridge Journal of Education* 30:1. 2000: 57–74.

Kress, G., *Before Writing: Rethinking the Paths to Literacy*. London and New York: Routledge 1997.

Le bambine e i bambini fra 5 e 6 anni delle Scuole dell'Infanzia Fiastri e Rodari del Comune di S'Ilario d'Enzo, Il futuro e una bella giornata ('the future is a lovely day'). Reggio Children 2001.

LeeKeenan, D. and Edwards, C., 'Using the Project Approach with Toddlers' in *Young Children* 47:4. 1992: 31–5.

Malaguzzi, L. *et al.*, *L'occhio Se Salta Il Muro: narrativa del possibili Comune di Reggio Emilia*. 1984.

Malaguzzi, L., 'Your Image of the Child: Where Teaching Begins' in *Exchange* 3:94 1994.

Malaguzzi, L. (trans. Gandini, L.), 'For an Education Based on Relationships' in *Young Children*. National Association for the Education of Young Children. 1993.

Malaguzzi, L., 'History, ideas and philosophy', in Edwards, C., Gandini, L. and Forman, G., *The Hundred Languages of Children: The Reggio Emilia Approach*. Greenwich: Ablex Publishing 1998: 83.

Malaguzzi, L., '*La Storia, Le Idee, La Cultura*' in Edwards, C., Gandini, L. and Forman, G., *The Hundred Languages of Children: The Reggio Emilia Approach*. Greenwich: Ablex Publishing 2006: 83

Martin, D. and Evaldsson, A., 'Affordances for Participation: Children's Appropriation of Rules in a Reggio Emilia School' in *Mind, Culture and Activity* 19:1. 2012: 51–74

Mason, E., 'The House of Objects' in *ReFocus* 5. 2007.

Mitchell, L., 'Using Technology in Reggio Emilia-inspired Programs' in *Theory Into Practice* 46:1. 2009: 32–9

Moscovici, S. (foreword), Herzlich, C. (ed.), *Health and Illness: A Social Psychological Analysis*. London and New York: Academic Press 1973: ix–xiv.

Moss, P., 'The parameters of training' in Penn, H. (ed.), *Early Childhood Services: Theory, Policy and Practice*. Buckingham, Philadelphia: Open University Press 2000.

Moss, P. and Petrie, P., *From Children's Services to Children's Spaces*. Falmer, New York: Routledge 2002.

Moss, P., 'Bringing politics into the nursery: early childhood education as a democratic practice' in *European Early Childhood Education Research Journal* 15:1. 2007: 5–20.

Moss, P., 'Dedicated to Loris Malaguzzi, the town of Reggio Emilia and its Schools' in *ReFocus* 1. 2005: 23–5.

Munton, F. J., 'Research on Ratios, Group Size and Staff Qualifications and Training in Early Years and Childcare Settings'. Thomas Coram Research Unit Institute of Education, University of London 2002.

Munton, T., Mooney, A., Moss, P., Petrie, P., Clark, A. and Woolner, J. *et al.* 'Part A: Review of International Research on the Relationship Between Ratios, Staff Qualifications and Training, Group Size and the Quality of Provision in Early Years and Childcare Settings'. www.education.gov.uk/publications/eordering-download/rr320.pdf

Munton, T., Barclay, L., Mallardo, M. R. and Barreau, S., 'Part B: Adult: Child Ratios for Early Years Settings in the Private/Independent Sector: A Report of Empirical Research'. www.education.gov.uk/publications/eorderingdownload/rr320.pdf

New, R., Mallory B. and Mantovani, S., 'Cultural Images of Children, Parents and Professionals: Italian Interpretations of Home-School Relationships' in *Early Education & Development* 11:5. 2000: 597–616.

New, R., 'Reggio Emilia As Cultural Activity Theory in Practice' in *Theory Into Practice* 46:1. 2007: 5–13.

Pace, Emma, 'Exploring Shadow and Light' in *ReFocus*. 2005: 14–15.

Pace, E., 'Rethinking Resources' in *ReFocus* 7. 2008: 12–13.

Paley, V. G., *Wally's Stories: Conversations in the Kindergarten*. Cambridge, Mass and London: Harvard University Press 1981.

Papatheodorou, T., 'Seeing the Wider Picture: Reflections on the Reggio Emilia Approach' in TACTYC. www.tactyc.org.uk/pdfs/Reflection-Papatheodorou.pdf

Penn, H. (ed.), *Early Childhood Services: Theory, Policy and Practice*. Buckingham, Philadelphia: Open University Press 2000.

Penn, H., *Unequal Childhoods: Young Children's Lives in Poor Countries*. London and New York: Routledge 2005.

Putnam, R. D., 'Education, Diversity, Social Cohesion and "Social Capital"' at Meeting of OECD Education Ministers, RECHILD 2004. http://web.ccsu.edu/italian/Conference/reggio_aprroach.pdf

Reggio Emilia newsletter, Il Centro Loris Malaguzzi. First published 1999; new edition 2006.

Reggio Children 'The Infant-toddler centers and preschools of Reggio Emilia: historical notes and general information'. www.cor.europa.eu/pesweb/pdf/Reggio%20children (accessed 19 January 2012).

Rinaldi, C., (2006) In Dialogue with Reggio Emilia: Listening, researching and learning. Abingdon and New York: Routledge 2006.

Rinaldi, C., 'Teachers as Researchers' in *ReFocus* 3. 2006. http://emh.kaiapit.net/lifeexistencedeath/teacherresearcher.pdf (also published by the Merrill-Palmer Institute, Wayne State University).

Rosen, Harold, 'Stories and Meanings' in NATE (National Association for the Teaching of English) Papers in Education. 1964.

Schroeder-Yu, G., 'Documentation: Ideas and Applications from the Reggio Emilia Approach' in *Teaching Artist Journal* 6:2. 2008: 126–34.

Smidt, S., 'Report on Visit to Emilia Romagna'. Unpublished report. 1992.

Smidt, S., 'Reading the World: What children learn from literature'. Stoke on Trent: Trentham 2012.

Sully, A., 'The Role and Responsibility of Documentation' in *ReFocus*. 2008: 9–14.

Steiner, *On Human Values in Education*. Anthroposophic Press 2004.

Strozzi, P., 'Daily Life at School: Seeing the Extraordinary in the Ordinary'. 2001. http://emh.kaiapit.net/dailylifeatschool.pd (accessed 23 January 2012).

Tarr, P., 'Aesthetic Codes in Early Childhood Classrooms: section 3'. www.design-share.com/Research/Tarr?Aesthetic_Codes_3htm

Trevarthen, C., 'What young children give to their learning, making education work to sustain a community and its culture' in *European Early Childhood Education Research Journal* 19:2. 2011: 173–93.

Turner, T. and Wilson, D. G., 'Reflections on Documentation: A Discussion With Thought leaders From Reggio Emilia' in *Theory into Practice* 49:1. 2010: 5–13

Vecchi, V., *Art and Creativity in Reggio Emilia: Exploring the Role and Potential of Ateliers in Early Childhood Education*. London and New York: Routledge 2010.

Vecchi, Vea (ed.), *Theater Curtain: the Ring of Transformations*. Reggio Children 2002.

Index